A BLOCK-OF-THE-MONTH QUILT

Across the Wide Missouri

A Quilt Reflecting Life on the

BY **EDIE MCGINNIS** AND JA

KANSAS CITY STAR QUILTS
Continuing the Tradition

Across the Wide Missouri
A Quilt Reflecting Life on the Frontier
by Edie McGinnis and Jan Patek

Editor: Jenifer Dick
Designer: Amy Robertson
Photography: Aaron T. Leimkuehler
Illustration: Lon Eric Craven
Technical Editor: Jane Miller
Production Assistance: Jo Ann Groves

Published by:
Kansas City Star Books
1729 Grand Blvd.
Kansas City, Missouri, USA 64108

All rights reserved
Copyright © 2010 The Kansas City Star Co.

No part of this book may be reproduced, stored
in a retrieval system, or transmitted in any
form or by any means, electronic, mechanical,
photocopying, recording or otherwise, without
the prior consent of the publisher

First edition, first printing
ISBN: 9781935362531

Library of Congress Control Number:
2010931573

Printed in the United States of America by
Walsworth Publishing Co., Marceline, MO

To order copies, call StarInfo at (816) 234-4636
and say "Books."

KANSAS CITY STAR
QUILTS
Continuing the Tradition

PickleDish.com
The Quilter's Home Page

Dedication

To my family and friends. What would I do without you!
—*Edie McGinnis*

To all of our frontier foremothers — grandmothers and great-grandmothers — who left home with their families and moved out into the unknown. They were women who lived in log cabins and soddy houses, milked cows, raised chickens, planted gardens and sometimes helped defend their homes, all while raising families. I hope our quilts do them honor.
—*Jan Patek*

About the Photography

We were fortunate to find the perfect location for photography at The Pioneer Spring Cabin located at the corner of Dodgion and Truman Road in Independence, Missouri.

The cabin was built around 1827 on land at 131 East Walnut in Jackson County. In 1835, Henry Younger and his wife, Beersheba Fristoe Younger, bought the property and lived there until 1847. It is said their 7th child, Cole Younger, was born there. Cole later rode with Quantrill and the James gang.

In 1972, the cabin was taken apart log by log and moved from Walnut Street to its present location. Generous people have donated artifacts reflecting pioneer days. The cabin is open to the public weekdays from 10 a.m.–2 p.m. April through October.

Contents

About the Authors

Edie McGinnis

Edie McGinnis, Kansas City Star author, editor and consultant, contributes as a columnist on The Star's website, www.pickledish.com. She has been designing and publishing quilt books and patterns for the past 10 years.

Jan Patek

A fabric designer for Moda, Jan Patek has been designing primitive folk art quilts and publishing patterns and books for more than 20 years. Visit her at www.janpatekquilts.com.

Acknowledgements

Jackie Howell, Margaret Falen and **Brenda Butcher** — What a debt of gratitude I owe these ladies for their help with making blocks.

Brenda Butcher — Brenda is the talented friend that did the outstanding quilting on my version of *Across the Wide Missouri* and *Gone Fishing*.

Jan Patek — Thanks for partnering up on this project. It's been quite an experience to work in the Primitive vein of quilting.

— *Edie McGinnis*

Thanks to **Carol Debault** and **Teri Caldwell** for all the great appliqué work. And thanks to **Lori Kukuk** for working her quilting magic on my quilts. I wouldn't have anywhere near enough time to design quilts if it weren't for **Shannon Jenkins**, my webmaster; **Tara Parks**, my office manager; and **Tori Showalter**, our Girl Friday.

An extra special thanks to my co-designer **Edie McGinnis** for all of her hard work. And for coming up with the concept for the quilt.

—*Jan Patek*

We'd both like to thank the team who worked so hard on this book:

Amy Robertson — Amy is the artist that makes the cover of the book and the pages look so wonderful. Thank you, thank you, thank you!

Eric Craven — We're so grateful for Eric's artistic talents. He's responsible for the portraits and those placement diagrams we all find so handy.

Aaron Leimkuehler — Aaron has that perfect eye for capturing photos. He's such a valuable part of the team and this book wouldn't be what it is without his remarkable photos.

Jenifer Dick, Diane McLendon and **Doug Weaver** – Your support is invaluable. We can't thank you enough!

— *Edie and Jan*

Introduction

St. Louis, Kansas City and St. Joseph, Missouri, were gateways to the West for the wagon trains that headed toward the frontier. We've heard the stories of the brave men who crossed the wide Missouri River in their quest for new land or riches. We've seen artwork depicting the wagon trains loaded with goods and families.

But something is missing. We don't hear so much about the women who trudged alongside their men. It's probably not too romantic to think about the challenge of doing laundry along the trail, or mending clothes or burying a child in the wilderness and having to leave the tiny grave while they went forward.

One has to admire the fortitude and bravery of the women who helped settle the frontier. It must have been beyond difficult to leave their homes and extended families behind, knowing the chances of seeing their parents again were practically nonexistent. Many lived miles from their nearest neighbors and had no one to help when they gave birth or when someone was sick or injured.

Across the Wide Missouri honors 12 women. Some of them you've probably heard of, maybe the names Charley Parkhurst or Narcissa Whitman ring a bell. Some you may not have heard of at all.

The women's stories are sometimes tragic and sometimes funny. They went West by themselves or with their husbands to find better lives. Some went by their own choice, others were property to be dragged along whether they wanted to go or not. The one thing they all had in common was uncommon courage.

Jan Patek and I teamed up to design the main quilt for this book. We each added a few projects as well. We hope you enjoy the stories and make your own version of Across the Wide Missouri.

Located at the Pioneer Woman Museum in Ponca City, Oklahoma, the Pioneer Woman statue is dedicated to all pioneer women of the United States. It carries the following inscription: "In appreciation of the heroic character of the women who braved the dangers and endured the hardships incident to daily life of the pioneer and homesteader in this country." Photo courtesy of the Oklahoma Historical Society.

General Instructions for Across the Wide Missouri

80" X 96" FINISHED

Fabric and supply requirements

- 5¼ yards of tans for block backgrounds. These may be all one fabric or a combination of different fabrics.
- 3¼ yards of plaids for sashing. Use a variety of medium to dark plaids.
- 2 yards of red and tan plaid or red floral for outer border.
- ⅔ yard of fabric for binding.
- ½ yard brown for large appliqué elements in Blocks 2 and 5.
- 20 assorted fat quarters in lights, mediums and darks for appliqué elements or scraps. Scraps are small pieces no larger than a fat eighth.
- Embroidery floss in colors to match Blocks 4, 5, 8 and 10.
- Embroidery needle.
- ¼" and ½" Clover Bias Tape Maker for bias stems in Blocks 4, 6, 7 and border.
- 2½ yards 1" ecru rick rack if you chose to use it for the pumpkin vine on the border.

You need to add a ¼" seam allowance to all pattern pieces and appliqué shapes unless otherwise noted. When we refer to a "scrap," an eighth yard will be adequate.

Fabric

Use 100% cotton fabric. Cotton holds a crease well and allows you to turn under a sharp edge and doesn't fray. Jan washes all her fabric before using and puts a white rag or washcloth in with the dark fabrics. If the cloth is not white at the end of the wash, one of the fabrics has bled. Rewash and put a cup of vinegar in the rinse water or use Retayne.

Fat Quarter

A fat quarter measures approximately 18" x 22" and is ¼ yard cut from one side of the fold on a bolt of fabric.

Fat Eighth

A fat eighth measures approximately 9" x 22" and is ⅛ yard cut from one side of the fold on a bolt of fabric.

Thread

Use 100% cotton for piecing and appliqué. Avoid polyester, as it will eventually cut the fibers of your fabric. For appliqué, use thread that matches the appliqué, not the background. Slide your thread through beeswax or products such as Thread Heaven if you have trouble with the thread knotting.

Above: Across the Wide Missouri. Quilt made by Edie McGinnis,
Margaret Falen, Jackie Howell and Brenda Butcher. Quilted by Brenda Butcher.

Above: Across the Wide Missouri. Quilt made by Jan Patek, Carol Debault and Terri Caldwell. Quilted by Lori Kukuk.

Needles

Use milliners, sharps or straw needles for needle turn appliqué. The larger the number on the needle packet, the thinner the needle will be. Jan likes to use milliner #9 with large eyes as they are easier to thread.

Pins

Use silk pins for appliqué. They're sharp and thin and pierce the fabric easily. A water soluble glue stick is also great for positioning the appliqué pieces onto the background.

Batting

We prefer cotton batting as it is thin and gives your quilts that "old" look. It is great for machine and hand quilting.

Marking Surface

Glue fine sandpaper to the back of a piece of masonite or cardboard. This makes a great board on which to mark your fabric and prevents fabric stretching and keeps templates from sliding. Mark on the right side of your fabric for appliqué and machine piecing. Mark on the wrong side of your fabric for hand piecing.

Freezer Paper Appliqué

Draw on the matte side of the freezer paper or the shiny side if you need the pattern reversed. Draw the templates the exact size without adding seam allowances. Cut out the freezer paper templates. Iron onto the right side of the fabric and cut out the pieces, adding ¼" seam allowance. If you iron templates onto the wrong side of the fabric, your pattern will be reversed. Mark around the templates with colored pencil or chalk. This line will help you know where to needle turn. Jan likes to use a sandpaper board to help hold the fabric in place while she's tracing around the shapes. Peel off the freezer paper.

Freezer paper appliqué templates are reusable. Place the shapes on the background. Pin, glue stick or baste the shapes into place on the background

Invisible Machine Appliqué

Trace the appliqué patterns onto the matte side of the freezer paper. After cutting out the pieces, pin each to the reverse side of the fabric you are using. The shiny side of the freezer paper will be up. Make sure you leave ¼" seam allowance around each piece. Press the seam allowance over onto the freezer paper to turn the edges. Remove the pins and then press each piece in place onto the background fabric. The waxy side of the paper will adhere to the background but you may need to use a pin for the larger pieces.

Stitch the pieces in place using the blind hem stitch on your sewing machine. Shorten the length and the width of the stitches so they barely cross over onto the appliqué piece. Match your thread to the appliqué piece rather than the background fabric. A 50-weight Aurifil thread works well for this.

When you have finished the appliqué work, make a slit in the back of the fabric and pull the paper out. You may want to use tweezers for very small pieces.

Berries

Trace the circle the required number of times onto freezer paper. Cut the circles out or use Avery dots. Cut the fabric circle ¼" larger than the pattern. (You don't need to be real precise.) Jan keeps her patterns and fabric circles in a Ziploc bag so she doesn't lose any. Make a knot in your thread and do a running stitch around the outer edge of fabric. Place the paper pattern inside and pull the thread until the fabric is snug around the paper berry. Backstitch and cut the thread.

Edie likes to use hole punches from a scrapbooking store when she makes berries. Using the hole punch eliminates the drawing step and avoids the tedious job of trying to cut perfect circles with scissors. Each punch is ¼" larger than the needed circle. Layer up to four pieces of freezer paper and punch out as many freezer paper circles as needed. For a firmer template, press two pieces of freezer paper together before punching out the circles. This technique works well for small berries and keeps the edges from crumpling over as you press (or glue) the edges onto the template.

Luzena Stanley Wilson

In a small cabin in Missouri, Mason Wilson had caught gold fever. He was determined to start out for California, leaving his wife and babes behind. Luzena, his wife, was not about to be left to fend for herself and the children. After all, how hard could it possibly be to ride in a wagon with two little toddlers?

The Wilsons sifted through all their belongings packing the items they felt were necessary for the journey in their covered wagon. They would need beds, pots and pans, clothing, food and, of course, the cow. They left their Missouri home behind without even bothering to sell the place even though they had labored for two years proving up the homestead.

Luzena soon found that many of the items she had thought were necessities soon became unwanted burdens. Kettles, pots and pans were dropped along the trail.

The trip was sheer drudgery. Luzena wrote in her journal:

"Nothing but actual experience will give one an idea of the plodding, unvarying monotony, the vexations, the exhaustive energy, the throbs of hope, the depths of despair, through which we lived. Day after day, week after week, we went through the same weary routine of breaking camp at daybreak, yoking the oxen, cooking our meagre rations over a fire of sage-brush and scrub-oak; packing up again, coffee-pot and camp kettle; washing our scanty wardrobe in the little streams we crossed; striking camp again at sunset, or later if wood and water were scarce. Tired, dusty, tried in temper, worn out in patience, we had to go over the weary experience tomorrow."

At the time she wrote this they had not yet reached the desert. They had been on the road for three months by the time they reached the alkali stretch that would take them three days to cross. All the water needed for the animals as well as the people would have to be carried along. Hot, thirsty and covered with dust, they struggled on. The oxen seemed to smell fresh water when they were five miles from the Carson River and picked up their pace. By the time they were within a half-mile, the dumb animals were running toward the water.

The worst of the journey was over for the Wilson family. Their clothing was so ragged it barely held together. The soles of their shoes had parted company with the tops making them virtually useless. But by the end of September they had found their way to Sacramento.

Luzena wrote:

"The night before I had cooked my supper on the camp fire, as usual, when a hungry miner, attracted by the unusual sight of a woman, said to me, "I'll give you five dollars, ma'am, for them biscuit." It sounded like a fortune to me, and I looked at him to see if he meant it. And as I hesitated at such, to me, a very remarkable proposition, he repeated his offer to purchase, and said he would give ten dollars for bread made by a woman, and laid the shining gold piece in my hand."

She had just made an amazing discovery. One didn't necessarily need to pan for gold. Sometimes it fell into your lap just doing your ordinary day-to-day chores.

Block One

21" X 12" FINISHED

Fabric needed:

- Background fabric
- Use the fat quarters for the appliqué elements or scraps of your choice

Cutting directions:

From the background fabric, cut

- 1 – 21½" x 12½" rectangle

- The templates are found on page 74. Cut out the appliqué elements, adding a ⅛" to ¼" seam allowance. If you need to cut more than one piece, you will find the number needed on the template.

- Refer to the diagram and appliqué in place using your favorite method. Leave an area about 5" square on the lower right corner to accommodate border appliqué elements that will overlap into this block.

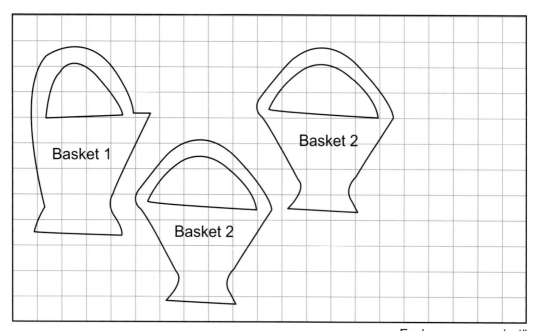

Basket 1

Basket 2

Basket 2

Each square equals 1"

Baskets were an essential household item for women on the frontier. Made of varying weaves and textures, baskets were used for many purposes such as gathering eggs and garden produce. Edie's block, top; Jan's block, bottom.

Bridget "Biddy" Mason

Bridget "Biddy" Mason walked from Logtown, Mississippi, to California eating the dust of every animal in her owner's wagon train. Robert Smith had become a Mormon convert and decided to move his entire family west to Utah in 1847. He gathered all his household goods (including his slaves of which Biddy was one) and set off on the 2,000 mile journey.

Biddy trudged on day after day trying to keep up with the wagon train while taking care of her three daughters, Ellen, Ann and Harriet, as she walked. One of her responsibilities was taking care of the herd of animals that brought up the rear. When the wagon train stopped for the night and others rested, Biddy had to keep on working. It was her job to cook, minister to the sick and do the laundry.

After months of hardship, they arrived in Utah and spent the next four years in Brigham Young's new Mormon community. In 1851, Smith packed up his household again and moved them all to San Bernardino, California. Smith failed to tell his slaves that they were living in a state that had entered the Union as a free state.

Biddy noticed there were many African-Americans going about their daily business, their own business, not some masters. She asked friends about the situation and found that she was living in a state where slavery was prohibited.

With the help of Charles Owens and Manuel Pepper, Biddy filed a petition with the Court for her freedom. Just being heard was a challenge since California law prohibited blacks, mulattos and Native Americans from testifying in court. It was impossible for Biddy to speak for herself.

In the winter of 1855, Smith again had loaded everyone up and was on his way to Texas, a slave state. If Biddy were forced to move there, her chance at freedom would be only a dream left in the dust of the trail. Before Smith could get out of the state, he was served with a writ of habeas corpus on Biddy's behalf.

Robert Smith failed to show up in court on the appointed day and Biddy was granted her freedom. Some sources say that all the slaves held by Smith were granted their freedom that January day in 1856.

Biddy moved to Los Angeles to live with the Owens family where she became a well-respected member of the community. She worked as a midwife and nurse and lived frugally. Within 10 years, she had accumulated the wherewithal to purchase a home of her own. In 1866, she spent $250 to buy a large parcel of land on Spring Street. Biddy had become the first black woman to own property in Los Angeles.

In 1884, Biddy sold some of her land for $1,500, and then built a building with rental spaces on the remaining land. Biddy, unwittingly, had just laid out the business district for downtown Los Angeles. She continued to buy and sell and invest in real estate. As the town grew, so did Biddy's holdings and net worth. She accumulated $300,000, which was a fortune in the late 1800s.

Biddy never forgot her humble beginnings and became a generous benefactor to many charities. She would open her pocketbook and help out churches in the community, regardless of the race of the congregants. She spent many hours visiting prison inmates and giving food and shelter to the poor. It was not unusual to see people lined up at her doorstep hoping for a little bit of help.

At the age of 73, on January 15, 1891, Biddy passed away and was buried in an unmarked grave in Evergreen Cemetery. Nearly 100 years passed before she was finally recognized for the brave, generous woman who had done so much and come so far in her lifetime. A headstone marked her grave for the first time and a year later a memorial for her achievements was built between Spring Street and Broadway.

Block Two

18" FINISHED SQUARE

Fabric needed:

* Background fabric
* 13" square for tree trunk
* Use the fat quarters for the appliqué elements or scraps of your choice

Cutting directions:

From the background fabric, cut

* 1 – 18½" square.

* The templates are found on pages 75-77. Cut out the appliqué elements, adding a ⅛" to ¼" seam allowance. If you need to cut more than one piece, you will find the number needed on the template.

* Refer to the diagram and appliqué in place using your favorite method.

Each square equals 1"

Settlers beginning a new life on the frontier often brought along farm animals such as chickens, cows, sheep, geese and turkeys. Not only were they needed for the new home, they also were a source of food for the journey. Edie's block, top; Jan's block, bottom.

Kate Carmack

In the 1800s women seldom got to marry their soulmates; instead arranged marriages were the norm rather than the oddity. Fathers and mothers were doing their best to look out for their daughters' welfare and, of course, with their vast experience and knowledge thought they could make better decisions than the average 14- or 15-year-old girl.

Tlingit Indians married off their daughters to prospectors to maintain control over trading. The Tagish controlled trade over the Chilkoot Pass, the highest point along the Chilkoot Trail between Alaska and British Columbia, used by Indians for trade and later by prospectors.

Kate Carmack, born Shaaw Tlaa, was one of eight children born of an arranged marriage. Kate had married a man from her own tribe and had a daughter. Sadly, both her husband and child died. Kate's sister had been married to George Carmack, a California prospector, and she had passed away as well. George had been living with his in-laws when Kate's mother insisted she follow Tagish custom and marry her deceased sister's husband.

Kate became George's wife and the two set off to try their hands at prospecting on the Yukon River. For the next five years the two lived off the land and tried to keep body and soul together. When they needed a little bit of hard cash, Kate sewed mukluks and mittens and sold them to other miners.

Seven years after they had married, Kate gave birth to a daughter the couple named Graphie Gracie. At the time, George and Kate were managing a trading post situated at the mouth of the Big Salmon River. In all this time, Kate had not been able to get back to her village and it was feared that the couple had perished.

Kate's family sent her brother, Skookum Jim, and her nephew, Dawson Charlie, to find her. The little family continued their nomadic existence and was prospecting in the Yukon near the Klondike River when they were found. There they had met another prospector who invited George to prospect with him on Rabbit Creek.

No one is really sure who found the first nugget, but both men staked claims on the

site that would become known as Discovery. It was the beginning of the great Klondike Gold Rush.

Kate had two strikes against her when it came to claiming a share of the gold. The first was that she was a woman, the second, she was a native. No claims were filed in her name.

Everyone worked the claim, but the winter of 1896-1897 was severe. The small group of miners was digging up thousands upon thousands of dollars in gold. Still they were far from trading posts and supplies. All that gold and they were suffering from hunger and lack of heat. It was a good thing that Kate knew how to snare rabbits and live off the land. She kept them all alive during the harsh winter.

The spring thaw finally came and George and Kate had collected more than $100,000 in gold throughout the winter. They stayed another year and continued to work their claim. The couple left the Klondike and traveled to visit George's sister, Rose, in Cambria, California. Rose didn't care for Kate, but she fell in love with Graphie Gracie.

The couple then moved to Seattle where George, never the shy, retiring type, rode around the town in his carriage. On the back of it he had mounted a sign that said, "Geo. Carmack, Discoverer of Gold in the Klondike." They were nearly responsible for a riot when they threw coins out of their hotel window one evening.

Kate was lonely, homesick and miserable living in Seattle. She turned to alcohol to deaden the pain of her existence and was arrested for making a disturbance in public. The Seattle Times jumped on the story and wrote, "Mrs. George W. Carmack, the Indian wife of the discoverer of the Klondike, who is probably the richest Indian woman in the world, was fined $3.60 by Judge Cann this morning for drunkenness."

George sent Kate and his daughter to live with his sister to get rid of her. He had become just as disenchanted with Kate as she had with him and her life. George went back to Dawson and fell in love with the owner of a "cigar store," Marguerite Laimee.

Laimee was a woman of ill-repute whose "cigar store" was a front for her brothel, her main source of income. Marguerite's business and her reputation didn't bother Carmack. He wanted the woman for his wife and set out to get rid of Kate.

He sent a letter to Rose and told her to send Kate and Graphie back to her people. Kate refused to be shoved out and made a bid for her share of the wealth. After filing for divorce, she found that no marriage papers had ever been filed. The court refused to recognize that a marriage had ever taken place.

Kate returned to her Tagish people and lived the rest of her days in a cabin her brother built for her in Carcross, Alaska. Her only income was that of a government pension.

Block Three

18" X 15" FINISHED

Fabric needed:

* Background fabric
* Use the fat quarters for the appliqué elements or scraps of your choice
* Use contrasting scraps for the heads, tails and fins

Cutting directions:

From the background fabric, cut

* 1 – 18½" x 15½" rectangle

* The templates are found on pages 78-79. Cut out the appliqué elements, adding a ⅛" to ¼" seam allowance. If you need to cut more than one piece, you will find the number needed on the template.

* Refer to the diagram and appliqué in place using your favorite method.

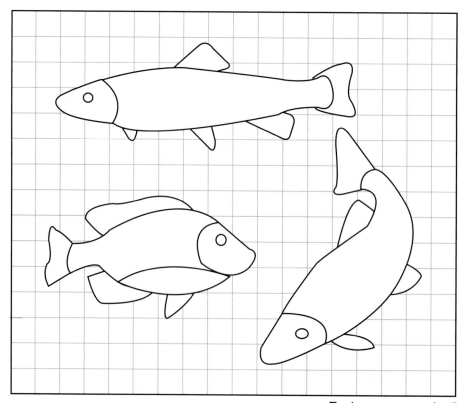

Each square equals 1"

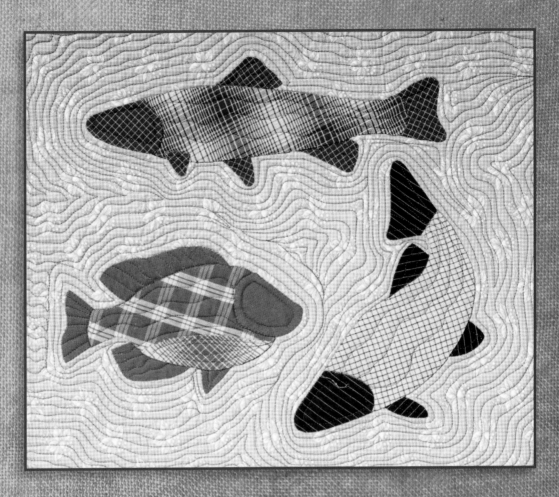

Fish were an all-important food source for people living on the frontier. It could be preserved using the sun and salt or packed in barrels of brine. Freshly-caught fish could be cooked quickly over an open fire and was a tasty change from the dried meat often used for meals. Edie's block, top; Jan's block, bottom.

Dr. Bethenia Owens-Adair

In 1854 at the tender age of 14, Bethenia Owens was betrothed to Legrand Hill. The marriage had been arranged by her parents after they had seen an ad in an Oregon newspaper posted by Hill declaring his desire to find a wife.

He was a handsome man and Bethenia trusted her parents' judgment. He and his parents had moved to Oregon and settled in the Rogue River valley, near the Siskiyou Mountains.

Bethenia wrote:

"It was now arranged that we should be married the next spring, when father's house was far enough completed to move in. During the winter and early spring, I put in all my spare time in preparing for my approaching marriage. I had four quilts already pieced, ready for the lining; mother had given me the lining for them all, and the cotton for two. I carded wool for the other two, and we quilted and finished them all. She also gave me muslin for four sheets, two pairs of pillow-cases, two tablecloths, and four towels. I cut and made two calico dresses for myself, and assisted mother in the making of my wedding dress, which was a pretty, sky-blue figured lawn."

Little did any of them know that Legrand Hill was probably one of the laziest men around.

Bethenia began her marriage with high hopes of living a long and happy life with her new husband. After the wedding they moved to a farm Hill had bought on credit. The farm was close to Bethenia's parents. Friends and family dropped in often and helped the newlyweds with chores and repairs to their little cabin.

Hill loved to hunt and was often gone from home extended periods of time. He began putting more time in on hunting than he did on doing his chores around the farm. The consequences of his actions were dire. He found he didn't have the wherewithal to pay the

$150 mortgage on the farm and he and Bethenia were forced to sell. They moved to Jackson County, Oregon, and lived with Legrand's Aunt Kelly.

Bethenia gave birth to a son, George, less than a year after the wedding. Now Legrand had a son as well as a wife but seemed no more eager to become a responsible father than he was inclined to be a responsible husband.

Bethenia's parents came for a visit and were upset to find the poor circumstances in which their daughter and grandson found themselves. Her father, Thomas, offered Legrand an acre of land and the materials to build a home if he would move back to Clatsop County.

The next few years were a case of parental rescue on behalf of Bethenia and her child. Back and forth they went always expecting Legrand to work and support his family until the day finally came when he tossed his son onto a bed in a fit of rage. Bethenia left and refused to return. After suffering for four years at the hands of her worthless husband, she filed for divorce.

She and her child thrived while in her parents keeping. Unlike Legrand, Bethenia was a hard worker. She held down several jobs in order to support herself and her son. Not only did she work, but she went back to school as well.

She had a good head for business and opened her own dressmaking shop and was able to send George to college and then on to medical school. Bethenia borrowed money so she could go to medical school herself. She graduated with a degree in hydropathy from Philadelphia, then went on to further her education in Chicago and Michigan.

After traveling the world, she returned to Oregon and opened up her own practice in 1883. Bethenia, who would remarry (and get divorced), became the first woman doctor in the state of Oregon.

Block Four

15" X 21" FINISHED

Fabric needed:

- Background fabric
- 1 – 8½" x 9" piece for bee skep
- Use the fat quarters for the appliqué elements or scraps of your choice
- 10" square for bias stems
- Embroidery floss

Cutting directions:

From the background fabric, cut
- 1 – 15½" x 21½" rectangle

- The templates are found on pages 80-82. Cut out the appliqué elements, adding a ⅛" to ¼" seam allowance. If you need to cut more than one piece, you will find the number needed on the template.

- Refer to the diagram and appliqué in place using your favorite method. Use the templates for the flower stems or make approximately 40" of ¼" bias. Embroider the details on the bee skep and yarrow with two strands of floss in a color to match.

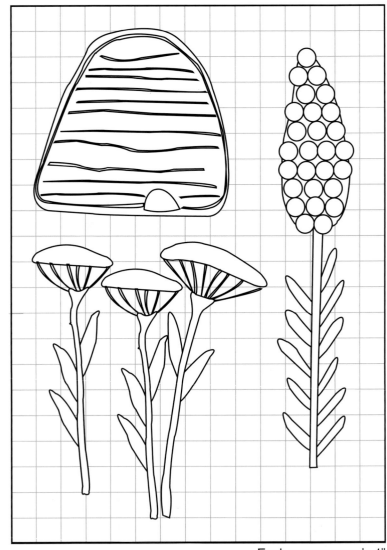

Each square equals 1"

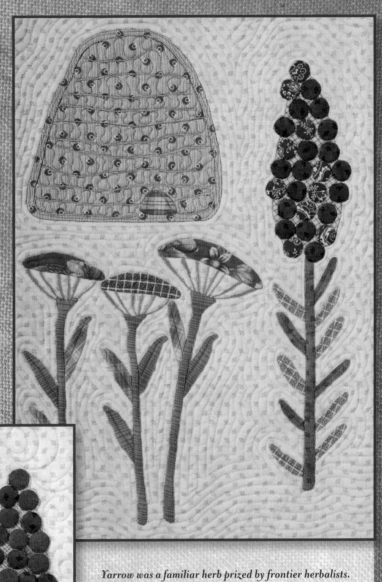

Yarrow was a familiar herb prized by frontier herbalists. Native Americans made tea from the plant to relieve fevers and colds. The tea was often sweetened with honey. The lupine was a plant one wanted to avoid. While a beautiful plant that attracted honey bees, it was also poisonous. Edie's block, top; Jan's block, bottom.

Narcissa Prentiss Whitman

Born March 14, 1808, in Prattsburg, New York, Narcissa Prentiss Whitman, was the third eldest of nine children. Her family was devout Presbyterians but when she was 11 years old, Narcissa converted to the Congregationalist faith. At the age of 16, she decided to become a missionary to the Native Americans.

She applied to the American Board of Commissioners for Foreign Missions but was turned away. The Board refused to send any unmarried person, male or female, out to foreign lands beyond the Mississippi River.

A doctor, Marcus Whitman, was in the same dilemma. He too had a burning desire to bring The Word to the savage peoples. When he heard about Narcissa, he began to write to her. Eventually he proposed marriage.

Dr. Whitman had already made one trip out West with another missionary and was familiar with the trail. He and his new bride set off for the West with another newlywed couple, Henry and Eliza Spalding.

It took the travelers five months to reach the fort at Walla Walla, an outpost of the Hudson Bay Fur Company. The couples settled about 25 miles from the fort in Waiilatpu. Narcissa and Eliza were the first two white women to travel the Oregon Trail.

The missionaries received a warm welcome from the Nez Perce and the Cayuse. The tribes lived a nomadic lifestyle and went where game could be found.

After building a home and outbuildings, the Whitmans and the Spaldings set about their work of converting the Natives. It was a clash of cultures. The missionaries encouraged the Natives to adopt a lifestyle that included staying in one place and becoming farmers. Neither Narcissa nor Marcus bothered to learn the language of the people they were trying to teach.

Narcissa often lamented the lack of privacy at the mission. The Nez Perce thought it was just fine if they came and went without invitation. Whitman thought they made far too much work for her as she had to clean up after them every time they entered her home.

On March 14, 1837, her 29th birthday, Narcissa delivered a little girl she and Marcus named Alice Clarissa after their mothers. She was the first white child born in Oregon County. Narcissa wrote to her mother and told her what a quiet child Alice was. The next letter to her family was filled with the agony of having to report on the death of the toddler.

> *"June 25th, 1839*
> *My Dear Sister:*
> *Your letter of April inst. I received but a few days ago, or it would have been answered much sooner. You make some important inquiries concerning my treatment of my precious child, Alice Clarissa, now laying by me a lifeless lump of clay. Yes, of her I loved and watched so tenderly, I am bereaved. My Jesus in love to her and us has taken her to himself.*
> *Last Sabbath, blooming in health, cheerful, and happy in herself and in the society of her much loved parents, yet in one moment she disappeared, went to the river with two cups to get some water for the table, fell in and was drowned."*

Whitman fell into a deep depression after losing her daughter. She whiled away much of her time writing about the events of her days and penning letters to her family.

The clash with the natives intensified when Marcus Whitman brought another large group of settlers west in 1843. Grazing land was taken away from the Natives and game became scarce with the additional mouths to be fed.

The winter of 1846 was particularly harsh and an epidemic of measles struck. The Nez Perce and the Cayuse had no immunity to the disease and many were lost. They accused the Whitmans of trying to kill them and steal their land.

The tense relationship turned violent on November 29, 1847. Several Cayuse saw Whitman getting some milk and demanded to have it for themselves. She refused, slamming the door in their faces. The Natives beat on her door and cried out for medicine. Dr. Whitman stepped out to try to calm the situation and was struck with a tomahawk. By the time it was over, the natives had slaughtered 13 people and taken 50 others as hostages.

After deciding that shedding more blood would not further their cause, the killing came to a stop but only after Narcissa Whitman was taken outside and chopped to pieces.

Block Five

24" FINISHED SQUARE

Fabric needed:

* Background fabric
* Use the fat quarters for the appliqué elements or scraps of your choice
* Embroidery floss

Cutting directions:

From the background fabric, cut

* 1 – 24½" square

* The templates are found on pages 83-87. Cut out the appliqué elements, adding a ⅛" to ¼" seam allowance. (The logs are appliquéd on top of the cabin base. Be sure to cut the base pieces that go behind the logs on the cabin.) If you need to cut more than one piece, you will find the number needed on the template.

* Refer to the diagram and appliqué in place using your favorite method. Embroider the sashing for the cabin windows with two strands of floss in a color to match. **Note:** Edie fused the oak leaves in place and used raw-edge appliqué rather than trying to turn the edges under.

Each square equals 1"

The size of a frontier cabin could only be as long as the trees cut down to build it were tall. If one needed more space, a cabin with a dog trot was usually the answer. This type of home was built with a cabin at each end and had a space or breezeway between the two. A roof covered the cabins and the breezeway. Edie's block, top; Jan's block, bottom.

Mary Fields

Six feet tall, heavy and tough with a short temper, this pistol-packing woman was destined to become a legend in her own time. Born a slave in Tennessee in 1832, Mary Fields was owned by Judge Dunn and grew up on the Dunn family farm where she became friends with the judge's daughter, Dolly.

Years passed and emancipation became a reality. Most people who had been enslaved moved on and left the farms and plantations they had grown up on. But Mary stayed with the Dunns before leaving to join Dolly in Toledo, Ohio. Dolly had become a nun and was known as Mother Amadeus at the Catholic Ursuline Convent in Toledo.

When Mother Amadeus went to Cascade, Montana, to set up a school for the women and girls of the Blackfeet Tribe, Fields joined her a few years later. Mary's ability to handle six-shooters and a rifle made her the perfect candidate for the job of delivering freight for the convent as well as doing other heavy work such as chopping wood and carpentry.

Her temper got the best of her when one of the hired hands complained about her being paid $2 more per month than he. He didn't complain only to her in insulting language but also talked it up in the local saloon telling the other patrons his grievances. It was too bad, but he was bad-mouthing her in the very saloon she patronized on a regular basis so it didn't take long for word to get back to her about his slander.

Paybacks seldom turn out to be a good idea but Mary was determined to have her due. She set out to shoot him as he cleaned the privies. She missed and he shot back and the gunfight was on. Bullets flew and even though neither hit the other with a direct shot, one of Mary's bullets ricocheted off of a wall and struck the poor man, ruining the seat of his new trousers on which he had just spent $1.85 of his hard-earned money.

Mary was summarily fired by the Bishop while the hired hand was given a raise.

By 1895 Mary had found the perfect job. She became a stage coach driver and carried the U.S. Mail. Dressed in men's clothing, smoking a nasty, foul-smelling black cigar, she

earned a reputation of being one of the most reliable drivers around. She and her mule, Moses, got the mail through in spite of horrible roads, winter blizzards and summer heat.

It seemed like Mary could get the all-important documents through that were necessary for claiming land in an expeditious manner no matter the obstacles.

For eight years, she was known as Stagecoach Mary. Even though few give her credit for her achievements, her efforts greatly advanced the development of Central Montana.

After retiring as a stagecoach driver, Mary thought it would be a good idea to slow down a bit and do work that wasn't quite so wearing. At the age of 71, she opened a laundry service in Cascade. One of her customers refused to pay his bill after picking up his laundry. Mary didn't take kindly to the insult. When she met up with him in the local saloon, she went up to him and knocked him out flat with one well-directed fist to his face. She then announced "that his laundry bill was now paid."

Block Six

15" X 24" FINISHED

Fabric needed:

- Background fabric
- 10" square of green for bias flower stems
- 15" square of brown for bias raspberry canes
- Use the fat quarters for the appliqué elements or scraps of your choice
- Embroidery floss

Cutting directions:

From the background fabric, cut
- 1 – 15½" x 24½" rectangle

- The templates are found on page 88. Cut out the appliqué elements, adding a ⅛" to ¼" seam allowance. If you need to cut more than one piece, you will find the number needed on the template.

- Refer to the diagram and appliqué in place using your favorite method. Embroider or use the templates for the flower stems or make approximately 33" of ¼" green bias. Embroider or use the templates for the raspberry canes or make approximately 80" of ¼" brown bias.

Each square equals 1

Raspberries and blackberries grew in the wild and, for the settlers, it was a real find. But berry-picking held its own dangers and people found it was wise to go to the patch in pairs; one person to pick and one to watch out for bears. Edie's block, top; Jan's block, bottom.

Eliza Farnham

Men answered the call of gold by the thousands back in the mid 1800s. When news of gold being found at Sutter's Creek traveled back east, men packed up and left for California. Some traveled by wagon, some by ship and some on horseback. All had their dreams of making a fortune firmly in hand.

Some of the prospectors had families they had left back East but many of the men were single. The men worked hard on their claims, then came to town and drank and caroused, going from one saloon to the next. Arguments turned to fistfights, fistfights turned to gunfights. It was clear that the men needed the gentling influence of the fairer sex.

Eliza Farnham was one of a handful of unmarried women in the gold camps. Her husband, Thomas, had died of pneumonia while visiting San Francisco. As soon as Eliza received word of his passing, she left for California with her two sons, Charles and Edward. Everywhere she passed, men stopped to stare.

Eliza had often espoused her belief that women were the true "civilizers in a frontier society." She thought women were needed to change the rough and ready ways of the men of the camps. As she traveled back East, she resolved to bring single women to the frontier.

Eliza wrote an ad explaining her intentions to be posted in the New York newspapers. She also stated her expectations: Women must be of good moral character, over the age of 25 and needed to have $250 to help defray the expenses of the trip.

More than 200 women were initially slated to go to California with Eliza. A sudden illness made it impossible for her to make immediate arrangements and be in charge of the trip. By the time Eliza had recovered, only a few women were still willing to go.

Eliza and her ladies boarded the ship, Angelique, on April 15, 1849. Anticipation ran high among the miners back in California. Horace Greeley had written,

> "The mission is a good one, and the projector deserves success. The enterprise in which Mrs. Farnham has engaged is one which evinces much moral courage. . . . May favoring gales attend the good ship Angelique."

When Eliza stepped off the ship holding her sons' hands, she saw the streets lined with men eager to claim a bride. What a disappointment they suffered when only three young ladies followed her off the ship.

Block Seven

15" X 24" FINISHED

Fabric needed:

* Background fabric
* Use the fat quarters for the appliqué elements or scraps of your choice

Cutting directions:

From the background fabric, cut

* 1 – 15$\frac{1}{2}$" x 24$\frac{1}{2}$" rectangle

* The templates are found on pages 89-90. Cut out the appliqué elements, adding a $\frac{1}{8}$" to $\frac{1}{4}$" seam allowance. If you need to cut more than one piece, you will find the number needed on the template. For the broom handle, use the template provided or make 10$\frac{1}{2}$" of $\frac{3}{8}$" bias.

* Refer to the diagram and appliqué in place using your favorite method.

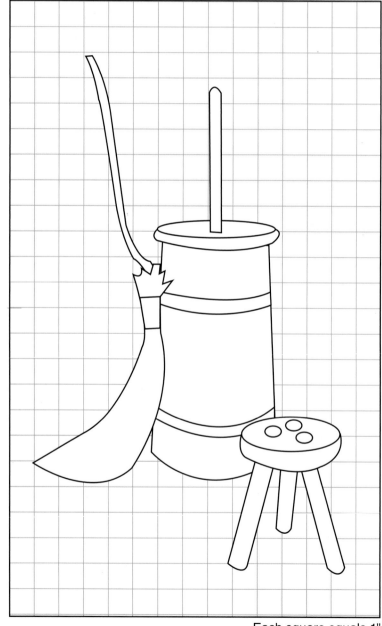

Each square equals 1"

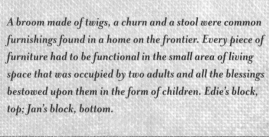

A broom made of twigs, a churn and a stool were common furnishings found in a home on the frontier. Every piece of furniture had to be functional in the small area of living space that was occupied by two adults and all the blessings bestowed upon them in the form of children. Edie's block, top; Jan's block, bottom.

Williana Hickman

Slavery had been dead for 13 years in 1878. Life was hard for the 4 million freed slaves of the South. Even though men and women could no longer be sold and families couldn't be split up on the whim of a master, they owned no land and had no skills other than those they had learned during their days of enslavement. Money was a rare commodity as was an education.

Little did Reverend Daniel Hickman and his wife, Williana, know that the opportunity to own land would walk through the door of their little church in Georgetown, Kentucky. It came during the winter of 1877-1878 when W.R. Hill visited the church and spoke to the congregation.

Hill was a white land promoter from Kansas. He painted a promising picture of the land to the west that was open for homesteading. Think of it, 160 acres per person! He told the parishioners of a town that was being incorporated by black people for black people. The town was called Nicodemus. To hear Hill talk, they could migrate west and live in the "Promised Land."

During the spring, the Hickmans set off for Kansas with their six children and 200 members of the congregation. The group split in two and headed out of the Kentucky hills for a new life.

They traveled by train for the first leg of their journey and arrived in Ellis, Kansas, a few days later. Tragedy struck many of the families as the children came down with measles. The Hickman family survived but two weeks passed while everyone recuperated.

The families then hired horses and wagons and began their final trek to Nicodemus. For two days they traveled across the prairie finding their way using a compass and vague landmarks. By the time they arrived at their destination, everyone was worn and weary.

Williana Hickman was 31 years old when she and her husband first saw Nicodemus. The reality was a far cry from the "Promised Land" she had expected.

At 90 years of age, Williana still recalled how she felt that spring day in 1878:

"When we got in sight of Nicodemus, the men shouted, 'There is Nicodemus.' Being very sick, I hailed this news with gladness. I looked with all the eyes I had. 'Where is Nicodemus? I don't see it.' My husband pointed out various smokes coming out of the ground and said, 'That is Nicodemus.' The families [there] lived in dugouts…The scenery was not at all inviting, and I began to cry."
—Topeka [Kansas] Daily Capital, 1937

For the next two years the community struggled and lived a hard-scrabble existence. Few turned back. They broke through the tough prairie and planted crops. Some managed to plant only an acre or two, others managed to till more.

The town grew as towns will. There was a post office, a general store and a hotel. Some of the buildings were built using native limestone but most used the building material at hand — sod.

Settlers cut strips of prairie that were about two feet long, three or four inches deep and about a foot wide. These "blocks" were stacked one on top the other much as bricks are laid. Most soddy houses had two layers of sod stacked side by side to create a double wall.

Soddy houses were preferred over a dugout since it was built above ground. But there were drawbacks to living in one. They were almost impossible to keep clean. Bits and pieces of the walls and the roof would crumble down. Rain saturated the roof and caused leaks and sometimes the roof would collapse.

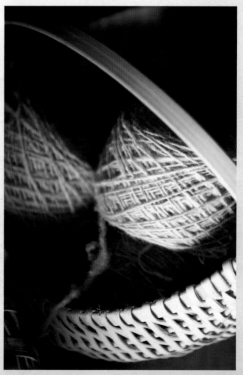

Bugs and rodents burrowed into the walls and snakes made themselves at home. Enterprising housewives put canopies over their beds so they wouldn't be surprised at "uninvited guests" dropping in while they slept.

Flea infestations were one of the most annoying problems. There were no remedies available for the "Kansas itch" so people scratched. And scratched.

There were pluses to living in a soddy house though. It was cool in the summer and warm in the winter. One didn't have to worry about their home burning when prairie fires swept across the plains.

None of the sod houses remain standing in Nicodemus. But then, they weren't meant to be lasting structures. For the people who had been slaves just a few years earlier, they represented a home – a home of their own that no one could move them out of or take away from them.

Block Eight

24" X 13" FINISHED

Fabric needed:

* Background fabric
* Use the fat quarters for the appliqué elements or scraps of your choice
* Embroidery floss

Cutting directions:

From the background fabric, cut

* 1 – 24½" x 13½" rectangle

* The templates are found on pages 91-92. Cut out the appliqué elements, adding a ⅛" to ¼" seam allowance. If you need to cut more than one piece, you will find the number needed on the template.

* Refer to the diagram and appliqué in place using your favorite method. Embroider the sashing for the cabin windows with two strands of floss in a color to match.

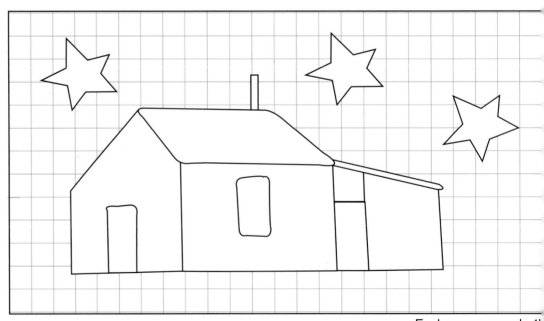

Each square equals 1"

Building shelter on the prairie required some ingenuity on the part of hardy pioneers. Digging a hole in the side of a hill and making a dugout was one option, cutting sod into bricks was another, especially if one wanted to live above ground. Both options came with its share of bugs and snakes and other uninvited guests. Edie's block, top; Jan's block, bottom.

Charley Darkey Parkhurst

Charley Parkhurst was one of the most talented, daring stagecoach drivers Wells Fargo had ever hired.

In 1851, Parkhurst migrated to California from New Hampshire. He was 40 years old when he landed in San Francisco. As he got off the ship he was wearing gloves and a pleated shirt. He was nearly 5 feet tall and weighed about 175 pounds. People were struck by his thin falsetto voice.

He spent the next 15 years driving coaches in California and Nevada. As the years passed, he became widely known for his skill as a "whip." They say he could slice a cigar right out of a man's mouth from 15 feet away using his whip.

Stagecoach drivers faced many dangers as they carried their passengers and cargo across the rugged terrain. Not the least of these was the hazard of highwaymen lying in wait to rob the stage. Generally the thieves would hide behind some trees then jump in front of the stage with their guns at the ready. While the passengers were seldom hurt, they were relieved of their cash and jewelry or any other valuables they had with them. The coach usually lost the box that held valuable cargo being shipped by the stage line.

Parkhurst had no patience with the thieves that tried to hold him up. When "Sugarfoot," a notorious bandit of the time, and his gang tried to rob Charley's stage, he left them in the dust rather than stopping. He cracked his whip over the horse's backs and raced off and began shooting at the gang. It was the last stage Sugarfoot ever tried to rob. He was found dead after having been shot in the stomach. Wells Fargo presented Charley with a gold watch in appreciation for his brave actions.

Charley had become a hero long before Sugarfoot tried to rob him. While going down Carson Pass, a rough, rocky road, the lead horse stumbled. Charley chomped down on his cigar and did his best to stop the out of control coach. His best effort was to no avail though. One of the wheels of the coach almost shattered when it struck a rocky embankment. Even though Charley was thrown from the stage, he had the presence of mind to hang onto the reins and somehow managed to stop the panicky horses. All his passengers and his horses were safe.

By 1856, Parkhurst was driving some of the roughest, toughest routes through the boom towns of Gold Country. During these years, he suffered an injury dealt to him by his lead horse, Pete. He lost an eye as a result of being kicked in the face and thereafter wore a patch over it. People started calling him "Cock-eyed Charley" or "one-eyed Charley."

Charley was a civic-minded citizen and voted for Ulysses S. Grant in the 1868 presidential election. This was some 50 years before women were allowed to vote.

Charley finally tired of being a driver and opened his own stagecoach station. When he wearied of that, he sold his business then farmed and worked in the woods near Soquel, California.

The years passed, Charley grew ill and passed away close to Christmas in 1879. He was 67. A few days after his death, the Sacramento Daily Bee published his obituary. It read:

"On Sunday last, there died a person known as Charley Parkhurst, who was well-known to old residents as a stage driver. He was in early days accounted one of the most expert manipulators of the reins who ever sat on the box of a coach. It was discovered when friendly hands were preparing him for his final rest, that Charley Parkhurst was unmistakable a well-developed woman!"

People were stunned. They had known Charley for more than 25 years and never guessed she was misrepresenting herself. She was actually named Charlotte and had been raised unloved and unwanted in an orphanage surrounded by poverty. She had run away when she was 15 years old.

Dressed in boys clothing, she found work at a livery stable owned by Ebenezer Balch. Charley cleaned stalls, washed carriages and scrubbed floors to earn her keep. Balch found

he had a promising protégé on his hands and taught Charley how to drive. Charley was determined to become the best driver in the business and could handle six-in-hand horse teams.

There was much speculation about the reasons Charley might have had for keeping her sex secret. But Charley herself never divulged the reasons even to her long-time business partner and companion Frank Woodward. Reports say that Woodward was extremely aggravated when he learned of her deception.

Block Nine, Nine A and Nine B

BLOCK 9 – 12" X 25" FINISHED
BLOCK 9A – 6" X 9" FINISHED • BLOCK 9B – 6" X 12" FINISHED

Fabric needed:

* 3 different background fabrics
* Use the fat quarters for the appliqué elements or scraps of your choice

Block 9 elements:

Along with this block we will be making two filler blocks, called 9a and 9b. They both use the same elements as block 9.

Cutting directions:

From the background fabrics, cut

* $1 – 12\frac{1}{2}"$ x $25\frac{1}{2}"$ rectangle for block 9
* $1 – 6\frac{1}{2}"$ x $9\frac{1}{2}"$ rectangle for block 9a
* $1 – 6\frac{1}{2}"$ x $12\frac{1}{2}"$ rectangle for block 9b

* The templates are found on pages 93-94. Cut out the appliqué elements, adding a $\frac{1}{8}"$ to $\frac{1}{4}"$ seam allowance. If you need to cut more than one piece, you will find the number needed on the template.

* Refer to the diagram and appliqué in place using your favorite method.

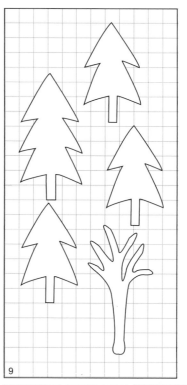

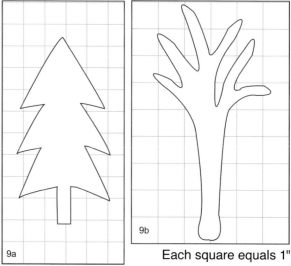

Each square equals 1"

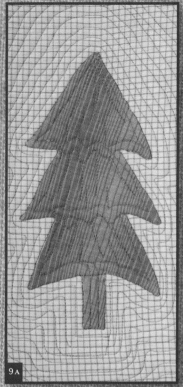

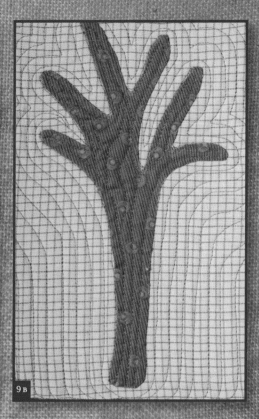

Tall hardwoods and pines were the silent sentinels of land some of the settlers came upon after crossing the dessert in their covered wagons. They were a welcome sight to homesteaders as a source of building materials. Women were especially grateful to be able to use wood rather than "buffalo chips" for their cooking fires. Edie's blocks, top; Jan's blocks, bottom.

Eleanor Berry

Lonesome miner wants wife to share stake and prospects. Please respond to Louis Dreibelbis in Grass Valley, California.
San Franciso Magazine
April 12, 1873

So read the ad 22-year-old Eleanor Berry of Gilroy, California, responded to in a respected literary journal.

Eleanor was an orphan who had been taken in by her loving neighbors, the Eigleberrys, as a tiny infant. She became a schoolteacher when she grew up. With no prospects on the horizon and a fear of remaining single, she answered the ad.

Louis was thrilled to receive Eleanor's letter. When he wrote back, he described himself as being a wealthy man who was anxious to settle down and have a family. He thought Eleanor fit the bill. Surely a woman such as herself who was so interested in children would make an outstanding wife and mother.

Letters flew back and forth between the two and soon a mutual affection developed. After three months of writing, Louis proposed and Eleanor accepted. They agreed on a wedding date of July 27, 1873. Eleanor resigned as the town schoolteacher and packed her belongings and took the train to meet and marry her fiancé, Louis.

Eleanor suffered through the train ride in the July heat. At Colfax, California, she transferred to a stage coach for the remainder of her trip. Little did the passengers know that there was a safe that held $7,000 in gold hidden among their bags and trunks.

Eleanor passed the time chatting with the other passengers and daydreaming about her wedding. She read over the letters she had received and envisioned herself as a bride exchanging vows with her husband-to-be.

The stage came to an abrupt stop when four men wearing masks and carrying guns rode out in front of it. They shouted at the passengers to step away from the coach while leveling a gun at the driver's head. The bandits demanded the driver to give up the safe.

After trying to open the safe with a pick, the thieves decided their best bet would be to blow it open with gunpowder. Eleanor had her trousseau in a trunk that was right next to the safe. Before they lit the powder, Eleanor cried out and begged the bandit standing next to her to remove her trunk first. As he stretched his arm out to take the trunk, she noticed a long ragged scar on the back of the man's hand.

The canister of powder exploded and the bandits picked the gold out of the debris. It didn't take them long before they hurriedly rode away leaving the stranded passengers to their own devices. The driver checked over the damage and decided they could continue on their way. The driver deposited Eleanor at the cottage of her beloved after reporting the crime to the local police.

Louis' landlady explained that he had been called out of town but would be back soon. Eleanor refreshed herself with a long hot bath, then pinned up her hair and put on her wedding dress. She timidly walked to the parlor when she was told Louis had arrived.

He was a bit older than she had expected but still he was an agreeable looking man. She thought there was something familiar about his eyes but dismissed the idea as ludicrous. Oddly enough, he seemed surprised to see her.

The minister performed the wedding and asked the two to sign the marriage certificate. Eleanor went first then passed the pen to Louis. As he signed his name she noticed a long ragged scar on the back of his hand and immediately knew where she had seen it before. She screamed and ran from the room.

Louis realized she had recognized him and rode away, leaving the minister, the landlady and his new bride.

Eleanor spent the night sobbing and locked away from everyone. In the morning she denied having married Louis and returned to her home in Gilroy. She insisted to anyone who asked that he had not lived up to her expectations. Eventually the real story emerged and Eleanor became the talk of the town.

Humiliated and embarrassed, Eleanor made an unsuccessful attempt at suicide. She placed a handkerchief loaded with chloroform over her head. Her guardian found her in time and saved her life.

Block Ten and Ten A

BLOCK 10 – 21" X 13" FINISHED • BLOCK 10A – 15" X 6" FINISHED

Fabric needed:
* 2 different background fabrics
* Use the fat quarters for the appliqué elements or scraps of your choice
* Embroidery floss

Block 10 elements:
Along with this block we will be making a filler block called 10a.

Cutting directions:
From the background fabrics, cut
* 1 – 21½" x 13½" rectangle for block 10
* 1 – 15½" x 6½" rectangle for block 10a

* Templates are found on pages 95-97. The tree templates are found on pages 93-94. Cut out the appliqué elements, adding a ⅛" to ¼" seam allowance. (The logs are appliquéd on top of the cabin base. Be sure to cut the base pieces that go behind the logs on the cabin.) If you need to cut more than one piece, you will find the number needed on the template.

* Refer to the diagram and appliqué in place using your favorite method. Embroider the sashing for the cabin window with two strands of floss in a color to match.

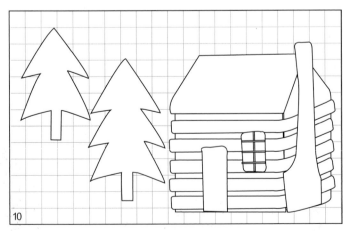

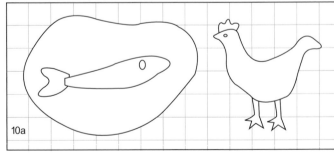

Each square equals 1"

Po
to
art

dea

ove
feve
sch
gath
and
actu
by U

C
oper
of 3(
hous

D
than
Phili

N
retur
him l
pover

Log cabins were traditionally small and could be built by one person who had a heavy axe and a hunting knife. The roughly hewn logs were laid out in a rectangle and jointed at the corners. The crevices between the logs were then "chinked" with mud and moss. Usually there was one door in the front and one window that was covered with greased paper. Edie's blocks, top; Jan's blocks, bottom.

Block Eleven and Eleven A

BLOCK 11 – 15" X 9" FINISHED
BLOCK 11A – 6" X 21" FINISHED • BLOCK 11B – 6" X 27" FINISHED

Fabric needed:

* Background for initial block
* 2 sashing fabrics for blocks 11a and 11b
* Use the fat quarters for the appliqué elements or scraps of your choice

Block 11 elements:

Edie and Jan put their initials in this block. Replace them with your initials so you can document your quilt and claim it as your own.

Along with this block, we will be making two blocks called 11a and 11b. They both use the same elements as block 9.

Cutting directions:

From the background fabric, cut
* 1 – 15½" x 9½" rectangle for Block 11

From the sashing fabric, cut
* 1 – 6½" x 21½" rectangle for Block 11a
* 1 – 6½" x 27½" rectangle for Block 11b

* The templates are found on page 98. The tree templates are found on pages 93-94. Cut out the appliqué elements, adding a ⅛" to ¼" seam allowance. If you need to cut more than one piece, you will find the number needed on the template.

* Refer to the diagram and appliqué in place using your favorite method.

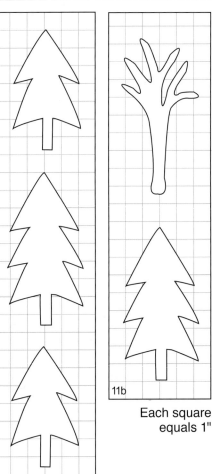

Each square equals 1"

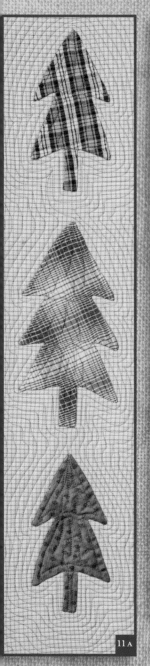

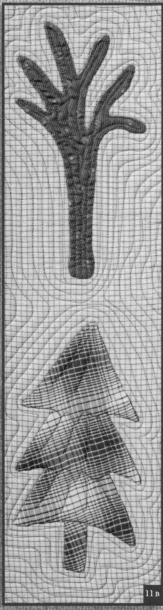

A land or mining claim was one of the most important documents a settler or a miner could hold in their hands. Proof of ownership was paramount for an individual who had staked out their homestead or their mining area. Edie's blocks, top left; Jan's blocks, bottom right.

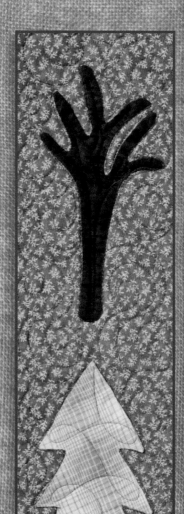

Louise Clappe

Louise Clappe's letters were published under the pen name of Dame Shirley.

In 1849, Louise Amelia Knapp Smith Clapp set off with her physician-husband, Dr. Fayette Clapp for California. He had been suffering from an upper respiratory illness and thought the fresh mountain air might help him recover.

Louise was a petite woman who had been educated in New Jersey. Well spoken and gifted, she crafted letters back East to her sister, Molly, who lived in Massachusetts. In her letters she gave a woman's perspective of the mining camps. The letters showed great wit as well as an appreciation of her surroundings. She always refers to Fayette simply as F.

Louise and Dr. Clapp sailed around Cape Horn on the ship, Manilla. Making up the party of four were Louise and her little sister, Isabella, Fayette and his brother, Alfred. The ship sailed from the harbor on August 10, 1849, and arrived in San Francisco January 10, 1850.

During the voyage, Louise's sister died and was buried at sea. In the 23 letters she wrote to Molly, never once did she mention this heart-breaking event.

Louise and Fayette stayed in San Francisco for a short time then moved to a mining camp called Rich Bar. Rich Bar was located in the Sierra Nevadas on the banks of the Feather River.

In her first letter to Molly, Louise wrote:

"I can figure to myself your whole surprised attitude as you exclaim, 'What, in the name of all that is restless, has sent 'Dame Shirley' to Rich Bar? How did such a shivering, frail, home-loving little thistle ever float safely to that far-away spot, and take root so kindly, as it evidently has, in that barbarous soil? Where, in this living breathing world of ours, lieth that same Rich Bar, which, sooth to say, hath a most taking name? And, for pity's sake, how does the poor little fool expect to amuse herself there?'"

Louise went on to tell Molly how poorly and sickly Fayette had been. He was sure he could recuperate and regain his health in the mountains.

The pair rode mules to their destination. They had gotten a late start from one stage and had planned to stop at Marysville around supper time. Louise wrote,

"...scarcely had we lost sight of the house, when all of a sudden, I found myself lying about two feet deep in the dust, my saddle, being too large for the mule, having turned, and deposited me on that safe but disagreeable couch. F., of course, was sadly frightened, but as soon as I could clear my mouth and throat from dirt, which filled eyes, nose, ears and hair, not being in the least hurt, I began to laugh like a silly child...But such a looking object as I was, I am sure you never saw."

Louise spent the next year along the Feather River using much of her time to write to her dear Molly. She told of the gambling, the drinking and the theft that went on in the camps. And she did so in great detail leaving behind an entertaining, readable record of what it was like to live in a mining camp.

By 1852, the prospectors claims were played out and Fayette and Louise left Rich Bar. In her last letter to Molly from Rich Bar, Louise wrote:

"My heart is heavy at the thought of departing forever from this place. I like the wild and barbarous life. I leave it with regret. The solemn fir-trees, whose 'slender tops are close against the sky' here, the watching hills, and the calmly beautiful river, seem to gaze sorrowfully at me as I stand in the moonlighted midnight to bid them farewell...Yes, Molly, smile if you will at my folly, but I go from the mountains with a deep heart-sorrow. I took kindly to this existence, which to you seems so sordid and mean. Here, at least, I have been contented. The 'thistle-seed' as you call me, sent abroad its roots right lovingly into this barren soil and gained an unwonted strength."

Louise and Fayette moved back to San Francisco and parted company. He moved back to Massachusetts and she stayed behind. She became the first schoolteacher in San Francisco. She divorced Fayette in 1858 and changed the spelling of her last name to Clappe.

She retired from teaching in 1878 and moved back to New Jersey where she died in 1906. Louise left a golden legacy in the form of 23 letters to historians.

Finishing and Border Appliqué

To finish the quilt, some additional piecing and appliqué is required. Below find instructions for piecing or appliquéing the flying geese sashing. Once the top is assembled, the border appliqué will be added to complete the top. The appliquéd tree blocks are already completed.

Sashing

Two methods are given for the flying geese units. Edie pieced the geese and Jan appliquéd them.

Pieced flying geese sashing

+ Make 47 – 3" x 1½" finished flying geese units. Edie used two different plaids for her sashing and a dark brown for her inner border. If you've used a different colorway, the background of your flying geese units should match the sashing strip to which they are sewn. You will need to determine the fabric placement for the sashing before making the flying geese units.

+ Use scraps from the appliqué elements and sashing fabric to make 22 geese with a red plaid background (or fabric to match your sashing) and 17 geese with a brown plaid background (or fabric you are using for your other sashing). Eight additional flying geese units made with the top inner border background (Edie used a brown background) will be reserved for the top inner border.

+ Cut 47 – 3½" x 2" rectangles from the fat quarter scraps. Make sure they contrast with the fabric you are using for your sashing.

+ Cut 44 – 2" squares from the red plaid or fabric you are using for your sashing.

+ Cut 34 – 2" squares from the brown plaid or fabric you are using for your sashing.

+ Cut 16 – 2" squares from the brown or fabric you are using for the top inner border. **CONTINUED ON PAGE 58**

Border appliqué for Edie's quilt, top. Border appliqué for Jan's quilt, bottom.

Finishing continued

Draw a line on the diagonal from corner to corner on the reverse side of all the squares. Place a square atop a rectangle and align the edges of the two pieces on the right. Pin the square in place and stitch along the drawn line. Trim the seam allowance to $1/4$", open the unit and press. Repeat with a matching square on the left side of the rectangle. Make sure you have a $1/4$" seam allowance across the top of the flying geese unit.

Appliquéd flying geese sashing
Make 42 flying geese triangles.

Use random scraps from the fat quarters to prepare 42 triangles for appliqué, adding a $1/8$" to $1/4$" seam allowance to the triangles. The template is found on page 102.

Refer to the assembly diagram on page 61 for measurements for the sashing that has flying geese units, and cut the sashing strips $1/2$" wider and $1/2$" longer than the measurements listed (use the measurements not in parenthesis). Refer to the photo of Jan's quilt for placement and appliqué in place using your favorite method. Make sure you leave a $1/4$" seam allowance on either side of the pieces and keep the points in the center of the strips.

Quilt top assembly
The following instructions use pieced flying geese. If you appliquéd your flying geese, skip the steps that refer to piecing the flying geese units to sashing fabric and sew to the blocks as noted.

Block 1 – Sew three flying geese together. Sew a $3^1/2$" square to the left and make sure the geese are pointing toward the square. Sew a $3^1/2$" by 14" strip to the right of the flying geese. Now sew this strip to the top of Block 1. Set aside.

Block 2 – Sew an $18^1/2$" x $3^1/2$" strip to the bottom of the block. Stitch Block 11b to the right side. Now sew 5 flying geese together all pointing the same direction. Add a 14" x $3^1/2$" rectangle to the bottom of the geese. We now have a strip that has five geese pointing up. Stitch it to the left side of the block. Set aside.

Block 3 – Two sashing strips are sewn to the top of this block. Sew 3 flying geese together to a 14" x $3^1/2$" strip. (The geese should be pointing toward the strip.) Sew the strip to the top of the block. Make the next strip by sewing 4 – $3^1/2$" squares together, then add a $3^1/2$" x $6^1/2$" rectangle. Sew this strip to the top of the block. Set aside.

Block 4 – Sew a $3^1/2$" x $21^1/2$" strip to the right of the block. For the sashing above this block, sew 4 flying geese together. With the geese pointing toward the left, sew a $3^1/2$" square to the right and a $3^1/2$" x $9^1/2$" strip to the left. Sew the strip to the top of the block. Make another sashing strip. Sew 5 flying geese together. Sew a $3^1/2$" x $4^1/2$" strip to the pointed end of the flying geese. This is the top of the strip. Sew a $3^1/2$" x 22" strip to the bottom of the flying geese strip. Sew this strip to the left of Block 4. Begin sewing at the bottom of the block and stop when you are within 3" of the top of the block. You will have a long strip dangling free. Set aside.

Block 5 – Sew one set of 5 flying geese together and one set of 3 flying geese. Sew a $3^1/2$" x $9^1/2$" strip between the two sets of geese. The geese on the left of the strip should be facing right and the geese on the right of the strip, should be facing left. To complete the sashing, sew a $3^1/2$" x $6^1/2$" strip to the right (the end that has the three geese facing left). Align the strip to the left side of the block and pin to the top of the block. You will notice it is longer than the block. That's okay. You are going to need that length. Begin sewing at the left of the block. Stitch until you have reached a point that is about 3" from the end of the block and stop. You will have some of the strip dangling free. Now sew Block 11a to the left side of the block.

To make the bottom sashing, sew three flying geese together. Sew a 6½" x 3½" strip to the right. The geese should be pointing toward the left. Now sew a 3½" x 20" strip to the left. The geese will be pointing toward this strip. Sew the strip to the bottom of the block. Set aside.

Block 6 – Sew Block 10a to the top of Block 6. Set aside.

Block 7 – Sew a 3½" x 24½" strip to the left side of the block. Set aside.

Block 8 – Sew 5 – 3½" squares together into a strip. Add a 3½" x 9½" strip to the left side of the squares. Sew this sashing to the bottom of Block 8. Set aside.

Block 9 – Sew a 3½" x 12½" strip to the top of the block. Add a 3½" x 28½" strip to the right side. Sew 3 flying geese together and sew them to a 3½" x 24" strip. The geese should be pointing up. Sew the strip to the left of Block 9 and set aside.

Block 10 – Sew 5 flying geese together. Sew a 3½" square to the left end and a 3½" x 11" strip to the right. The geese will be pointing toward the right. Sew the strip to the top of the block.

Block 11 – Sew Block 9a to the right side of Block 11. Sew these to the top of Block 10. Now stitch a 3½" x 25½" strip to the left side of the Block 10/Block 11 unit. Sew a 24½" x 3½" strip to the bottom of this unit. Pick up Block 9 and stitch it on to the right.

Sew the Block 6/Block 10a unit to the left side of Block 5. Then sew Block 3 to left side of Block 2. Join these two blocks together with 2 and 3 on the bottom. Refer to the photo if necessary.

Sew Block 7 to the top of Block 4. (Remember, that strip of sashing on the side of Block 4 is supposed to be hanging loose.) Then sew Block 1 to the bottom of Block 4.

◆ Go back and stitch Block 9b to Block 7. Begin sewing at the top of Block 7 and sew to within 2" or 3" of the bottom of Block 9b and stop. (There will still be open seams.)

◆ Sew Block 8 on the top of Block 9b and Block 7. Stitch the Block 9/10/11 unit to the Block 8/9b unit. Now stitch the unit made up of Blocks 10a/5/6/3/2 together in place. Refer to the diagram. Now go back and close up the seam under Block 9b. Then close up the seam between Block 7 and 5.

Inner borders

◆ Cut 1 – 3½" x 79½" strip for the side inner border. Sew to the left side of the quilt top.

◆ For the top inner border, sew 5 flying geese together, pointing toward the left. Add a 3½" x 15" strip to the left of the geese. Add 3 flying geese pointing to the left again. Now add a 3½" x 43" strip to the pointed side of the geese. Sew to the top of the quilt top.

◆ Cut 1 – 3½" x 69½" strip for the bottom inner border. Sew to the bottom of the quilt top.

Outer border

◆ Cut 1 – 7½" x 69½" strip and sew it to the bottom of the quilt.

◆ Cut 1 – 4½" x 69½" strip and sew it to the top of the quilt.

◆ Cut 1 – 4½" x 96½" strip and sew it to the left side of the quilt.

◆ Cut 1 – 7½" x 96½" strip and sew it to the right side of the quilt. CONTINUED ON PAGE 60

Finishing continued

Border Appliqué

The templates are found on pages 99-102. Using the
fat quarters for the appliqué elements or scraps of your
choice, cut out the appliqué elements, adding a $\frac{1}{8}$" to
$\frac{1}{4}$" seam allowance. You will find the number of pieces
needed on the templates. Make approximately 80" of $\frac{1}{2}$"
finished bias or use ecru 1" rick rack for the pumpkin vine.
Appliqué in place using your favorite method.

Each square equals 1"

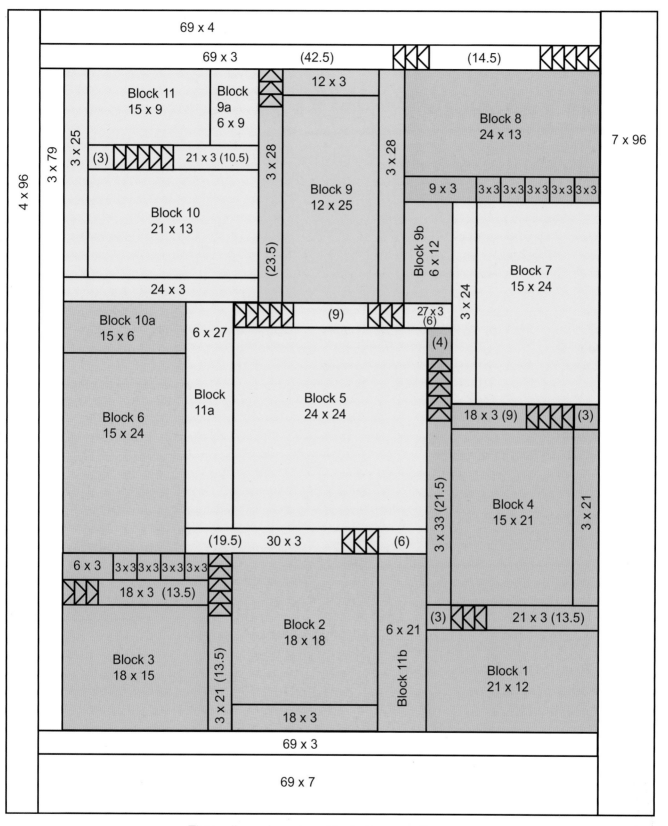

69 x 4

69 x 3 (42.5) (14.5)

4 x 96

3 x 79

7 x 96

3 x 25

Block 11
15 x 9

Block
9a
6 x 9

12 x 3

Block 8
24 x 13

(3) 21 x 3 (10.5)

3 x 28

Block 9
12 x 25

3 x 28

9 x 3 3x3 3x3 3x3 3x3 3x3

Block 10
21 x 13

Block 9b
6 x 12

Block 7
15 x 24

3 x 24

(23.5)

24 x 3

Block 10a
15 x 6

6 x 27

(9) 27 x 3
(6)

Block 6
15 x 24

Block
11a

Block 5
24 x 24

(4)

18 x 3 (9) (3)

3 x 33 (21.5)

Block 4
15 x 21

3 x 21

(19.5) 30 x 3 (6)

6 x 3 3x3 3x3 3x3 3x3

18 x 3 (13.5)

Block 2
18 x 18

(3) 21 x 3 (13.5)

3 x 21 (13.5)

6 x 21

Block 3
18 x 15

Block 11b

Block 1
21 x 12

18 x 3

69 x 3

69 x 7

These dimensions do not include seam allowance.

Summer Nights

69" X 78" FINISHED • BLOCK SIZE 12" FINISHED
BY JAN PATEK

Fabric needed:

For Star Blocks
- ¼ yard of 6 tans
- ¼ yard of 6 red prints

For Basket Blocks
- ⅜ yard of tan No. 1 for 3 backgrounds
- 2 fat quarters of tan No. 2 for 2 backgrounds
- 1 fat quarter of tan No. 3 for background
- 1 fat quarter of dark print No. 1 for 2 baskets
- 1 fat quarter of dark print No. 2 for 2 baskets
- 1 fat eighth of dark print No. 3 for 1 basket
- 1 fat eighth of dark print No. 4 for 1 basket
- 1 fat quarter of dark print or solid for basket handles and bases
- Scraps for flowers, buds, stems and leaves

For Setting Triangles and Squares
- 1⅜ yard of green print No. 1
- ⅝ yard of green print No. 2

For Borders
- ⅓ yard of blue print
- 1½ yard of dark print

Binding
- ⅝ yard of red

Templates

Templates are found on pages 103-104.

Cutting
Star Blocks

From each of 6 tans, cut
- 4 – 3½" squares
- 6 – 3⅞" squares. Cut in half on the diagonal to yield 12 triangles.

From each of 6 red prints, cut
- 6 – 3⅞" squares. Cut in half on the diagonal to yield 12 triangles.

Basket Blocks

From the tans, cut
- 6 – 12½" squares

Setting Squares and Triangles

From the green prints, cut
- 6 – 12½" setting squares
- 3 – 18¼" squares. Cut in half on both diagonals to yield 12 large side setting triangles. Reserve 2 triangles for another project
- 2 – 9⅜" squares. Cut in half on the diagonal to yield 4 corner setting triangles **CONTINUED ON PAGE 65**

Designed by Jan Patek. Sewn by Wendy Byrne. Quilted by Lori Kukuk.

Borders

From the blue print, cut

- 7 – 1½" strips. Stitch together and cut
  - 2 – 68½" x 1½" narrow side borders
  - 2 – 53½" x 1½" narrow top and bottom borders

From the dark print, cut

- 4 – 8½" strips. Stitch together and cut
  - 2 – 70½" x 8½" outer side borders
- 4 – 4½" strips. Stitch together and cut
  - 2 – 69½" x 4½" outer top and bottom borders

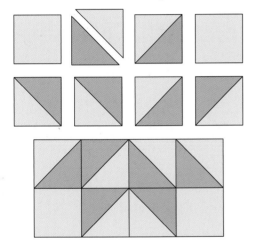

Star Blocks

Make 6.

- Make 12 half-square triangle units per block by sewing 1 light triangle to 1 dark triangle. Press to the dark.

- Lay out 4 plain squares and 12 half-square triangle units as shown in the diagram and sew together in rows. Sew the rows together. Press the seams to one side.

Basket Blocks

Prepare the shapes for appliqué using the method of your choice. If you prefer to use freezer paper appliqué, refer to the instructions on page 9. Lay out the shapes on the background fabric and appliqué in place.

Finishing

- Lay out the Star blocks, Basket blocks and setting squares and setting triangles in diagonal rows as shown in the quilt assembly diagram. Sew into diagonal rows. Join the rows.

- Sew the narrow borders to the sides first then the top and bottom. Press.

- Sew the outer borders to the sides first then the top and bottom. Press.

- Layer the top with backing and batting. Quilt and bind.

Gone Fishin'

51" SQUARE FINISHED • BLOCK SIZE: 12" FINISHED
BY EDIE MCGINNIS

Fabric needed:

- 3 yards dark blue (includes enough fabric for binding)
- 1¼ yards yard dark tan
- 9 fat eighths and contrasting scraps for fish

Templates

Templates are found on pages 78-79.

Cutting

From the dark blue fabric, cut

- 9 – 13" squares
- 4 – 2" squares for sashing cornerstones
- 4 – 5" strips across the width of the fabric for borders
- 1 – 2½" strip for pieced border

From the dark tan fabric, cut

- 9 – 2" strips across the width of the fabric for sashing, first border and pieced border
- 4 – 5" squares for borders

Appliqué

You will need to make three of each fish. Cut out the pieces required for the bodies from a fat eighth and use contrasting fabric for the heads, tails and fins. Prepare the pieces for appliqué using your favorite method.

- Appliqué one fish to each 13" dark blue square. After you have finished appliquéing the fish in place, trim the blocks to 12½". **CONTINUED ON PAGE 68**

Designed and made by Edie McGinnis, quilted by Brenda Butcher, Independence, Missouri.

Gone Fishin' continued

Finishing

- Cut 4 of the 2" tan strips into 12½" increments. You need 12 strips.

- Sew the blocks together into rows using a tan strip between each block. Make three rows.

- Make two sashing rows by sewing tan strips to blue squares. Refer to the diagram if necessary.

- Sew the rows of blocks to the sashing strips.

- Measure the center of the quilt from top to bottom through the center. Trim 2 of the tan strips to that length and sew one to either side of the quilt top.

- Measure the quilt through the center vertically and trim 2 tan strips to that length. Sew one strip to the top of the quilt and one to the bottom.

- Again, measure the quilt top from top to bottom through the center. Trim 2 of the dark blue 5" strips to that measurement and sew to either side of the quilt.

- Sew the remaining tan strip to the 2½" blue strip. Press the seam toward the blue fabric. Cut the strip into 5" increments. Sew three of these tan/blue units together. Make 2, one for the top border and one for the bottom. The units should measure 11" unfinished.

- Sew a tan/blue strip unit to a tan 5" square. Add a 5" x 32" strip of blue fabric. (You would be wise to measure your quilt top and make sure the 32" strip will be perfect.) Add a 5" tan square. Make 2 strips. Sew one to the top and one to the bottom of the quilt.

- Layer the top with backing and batting. Quilt and bind.

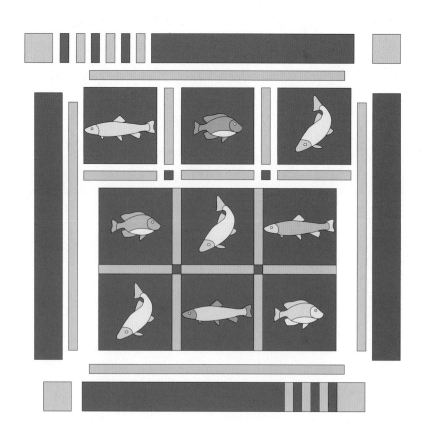

Church Bells in the Snow

45" X 46" FINISHED
BY JAN PATEK

Fabric needed:

Background

- ⅓ yard for sky (top background)
- ½ yard for church background
- ⅓ yard for right background
- ¼ yard for snow (bottom background)

Appliqué

- 1 fat quarter for church body
- Scraps for steeple, roof, windows and door
- 4 fat eighths for trees
- 1 fat eighth for snowman and angel body
- Scraps for angel head, feet and wing, stars, moon and bird

Broken Dishes Blocks

- ½ yard light print
- 7 scraps of varied dark prints or homespuns at least 4" x 8"

Borders

- ⅓ yard red print for right and top borders
- ⅓ yard plaid for left and bottom borders

Binding

- ⅜ yard

Templates

Templates are found on pages 105-111.

Cutting
Background

From the sky fabric, cut
- 1 – 10½" x 24½" rectangle

From the church background fabric, cut
- 1 – 16½" x 24½" rectangle

From the right background fabric, cut
- 1 – 9½" x 26½" rectangle

From the snow fabric, cut
- 1 – 4½" x 33½" rectangle

Broken Dishes Border

From the light print, cut
- 23 – 3⅞" squares. Cut each in half on the diagonal to yield 46 triangles.

From the 7 dark prints or homespuns, cut
- 23 – 3⅞" squares. Cut each in half on the diagonal to yield 46 triangles. CONTINUED ON PAGE 73

Designed and made by Jan Patek.
Quilted by Lori Kukuk.

Borders

From the red print, cut
* $1 - 4^{1}/_{2}$" x $41^{1}/_{2}$" rectangle
* $1 - 4^{1}/_{2}$" x $40^{1}/_{2}$" rectangle

From the plaid, cut
* $1 - 2^{1}/_{2}$" x $42^{1}/_{2}$" rectangle
* $1 - 6^{1}/_{2}$" x $43^{1}/_{2}$" rectangle

Main Body

* Sew the sky to the top of the church background. Sew the right side to this unit. Sew the snow to the bottom.

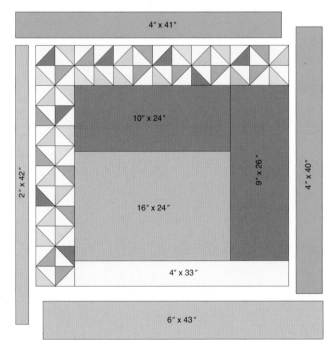

Note: Dimensions do not include seam allowance.

* Prepare the shapes for appliqué using the method of your choice. If you prefer to use freezer paper appliqué, refer to the instructions on page 9. Lay out the shapes as shown in the picture and appliqué to the main body of the quilt.

Broken Dishes Border

* Make 46 half square triangle units by sewing 1 light triangle to 1 dark triangle. Press to the dark.

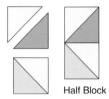

Half Block

* Referring to the block diagram, make 10 Broken Dishes blocks. Sew the remaining 6 half-square triangles together as shown in the diagram to make 3 half blocks.

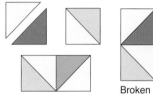

Broken Dishes Block

* Sew 5 Broken Dishes blocks together in a row to make the left border. Sew this to the side of the appliqué main body.

* To make the top border, refer to the diagram and sew together 5 Broken Dishes blocks and 3 half blocks. Sew this to the top of the quilt. **Note:** It helps to lay out each section to make sure it looks like the photo before sewing it together.

Finishing

* Mark the top red border at $2^{1}/_{4}$" from left side. Sew this border to the top stopping when you are to that mark. Leave this hanging loose.

* Sew the red side border to the right side of the quilt.

* Sew the bottom plaid border to the bottom of the quilt.

* Sew the left plaid border to the left side of the quilt.

* Now go back to the top border that you left hanging loose, and finish the seam.

* Layer the top with backing and batting. Quilt and bind.

Block 1

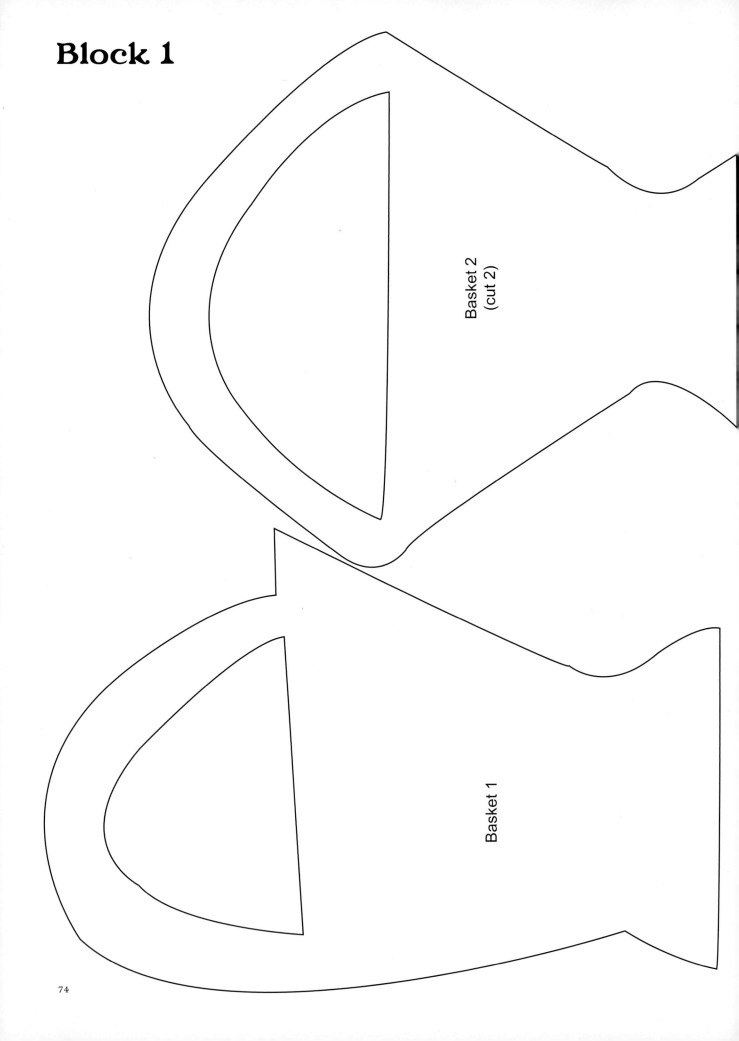

Basket 2
(cut 2)

Basket 1

Block 2

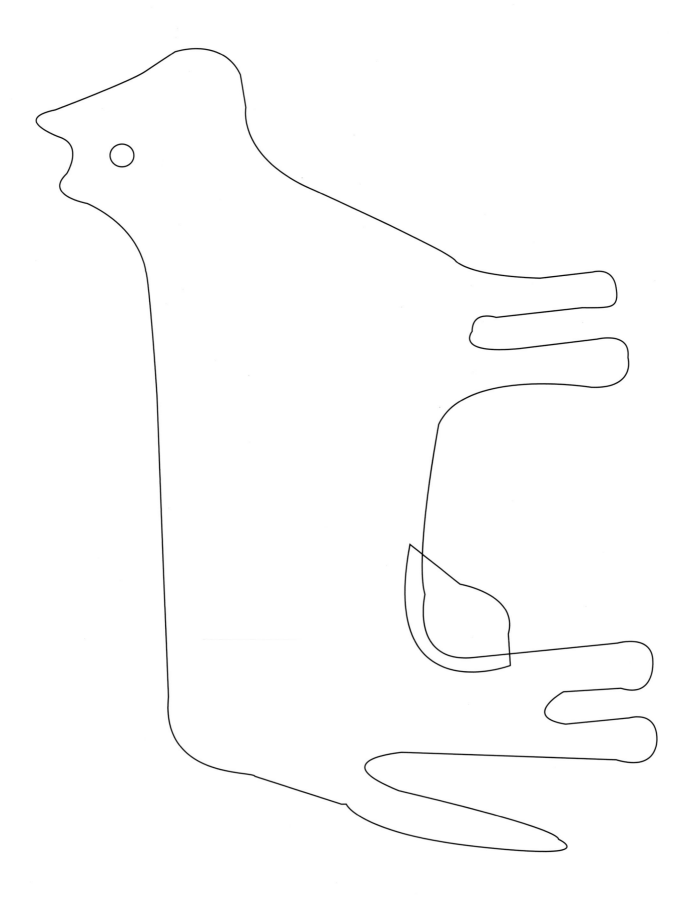

Block 2

Cut
30

Place on fold of freezer paper to make pattern for tree

Join the trunk at points A and B when making your freezer paper template. Refer to the placement diagram on page 16 if necessary.

A B

A

B

Place on fold of freezer paper to make pattern for tree

Block 3

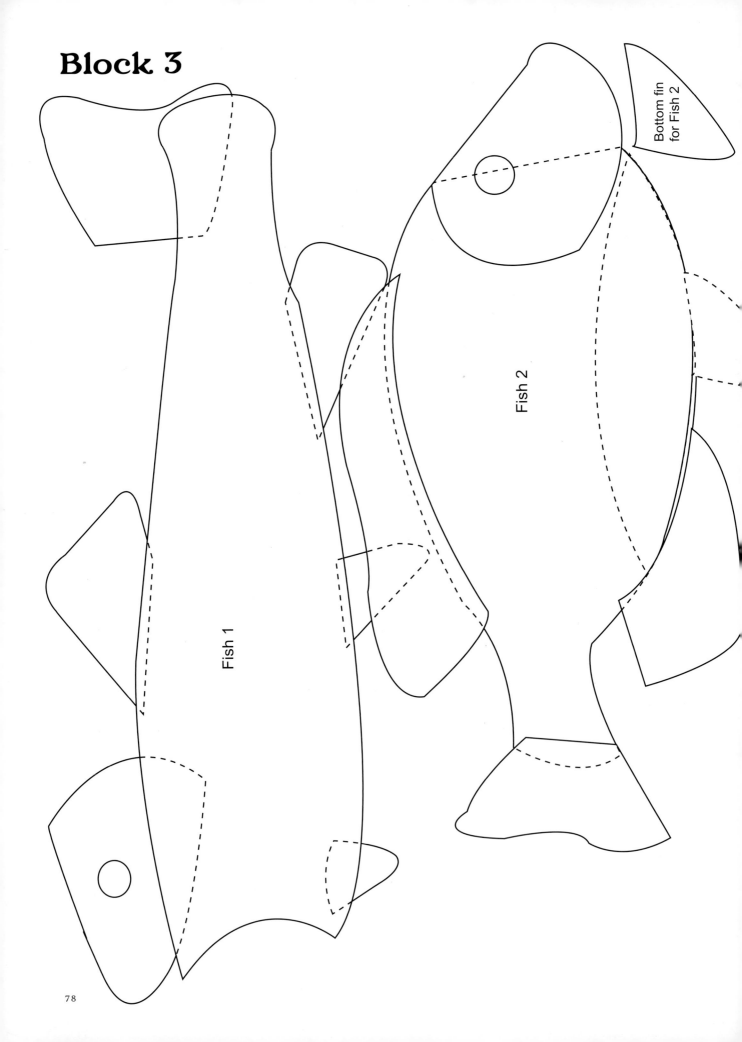

Fish 1

Fish 2

Bottom fin for Fish 2

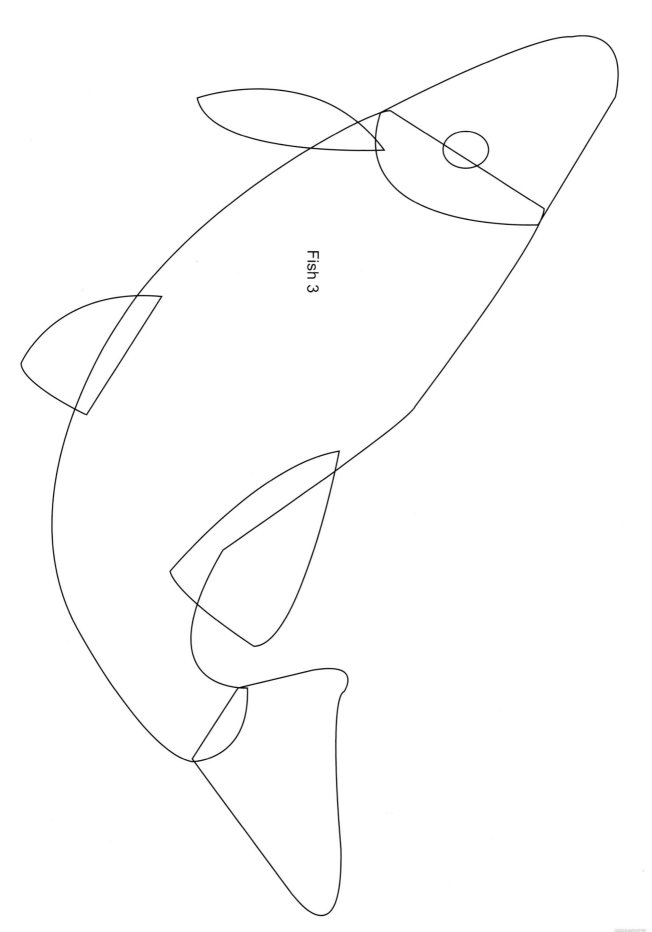

Fish 3

Block 4

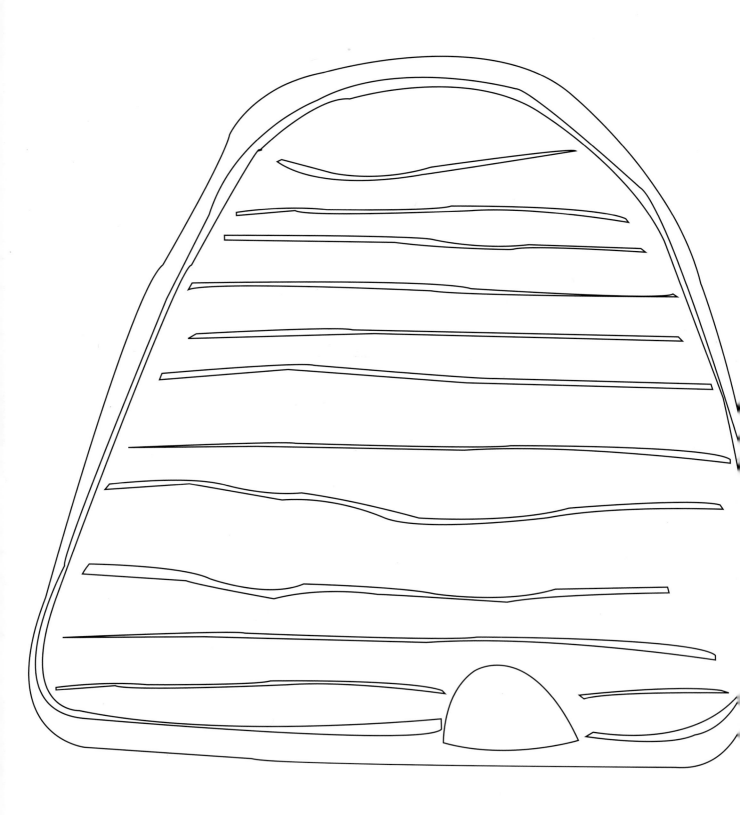

Cut 27

Block 4

Cut 2

Cut 2

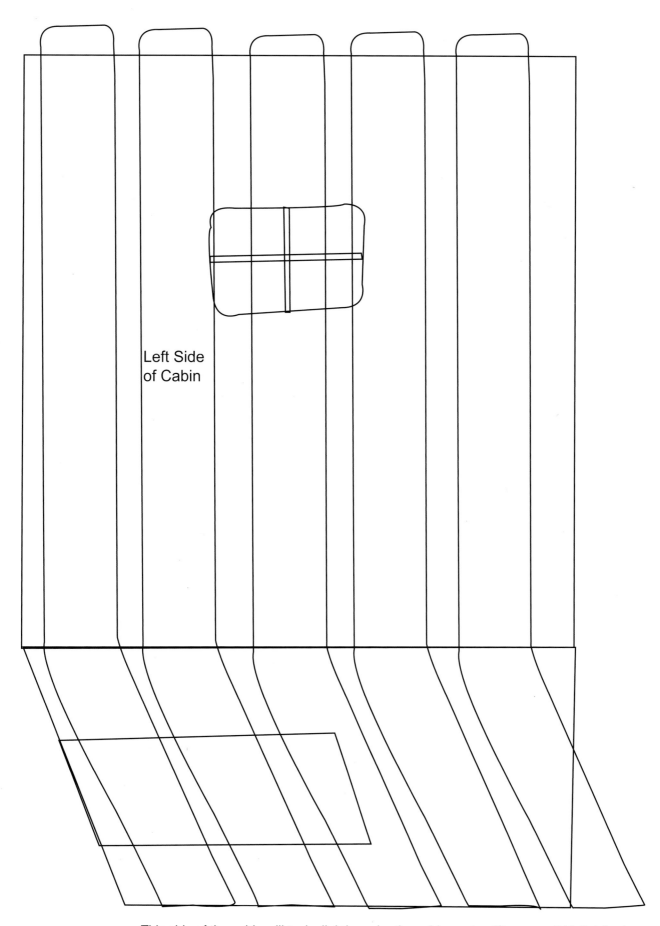

Left Side
of Cabin

Block 5

This side of the cabin will tuck slightly under the cabin center. (See page 84.) Cut the logs for this side of the cabin individually and appliqué them to the base of the cabin. Add the door and window last. Refer to the placement diagram on page 28 if necessary.

Block 5

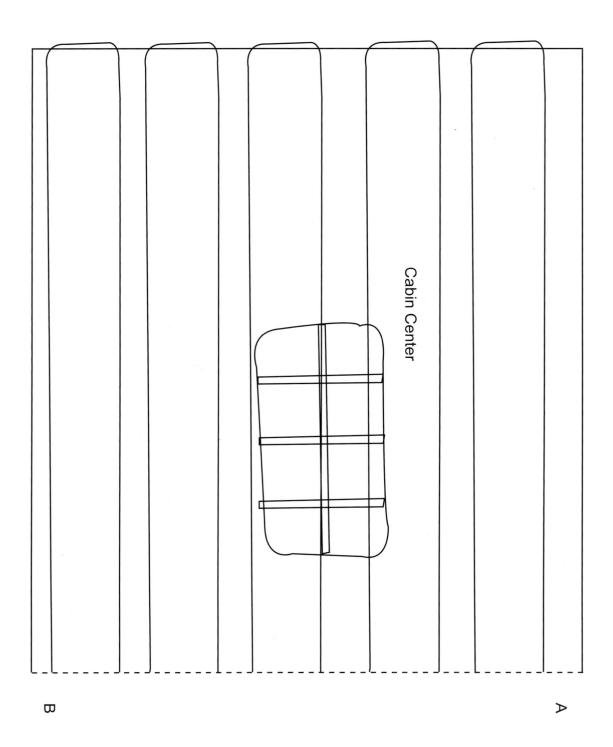

Cabin Center

B

A

Join the A and B points on this template to the A and B points of the
template on the next page when making your freezer paper templates.
Cut the logs individually and appliqué them to the cabin base. Add the
chimney and window. Refer to the placement diagram on page 28 if
necessary.

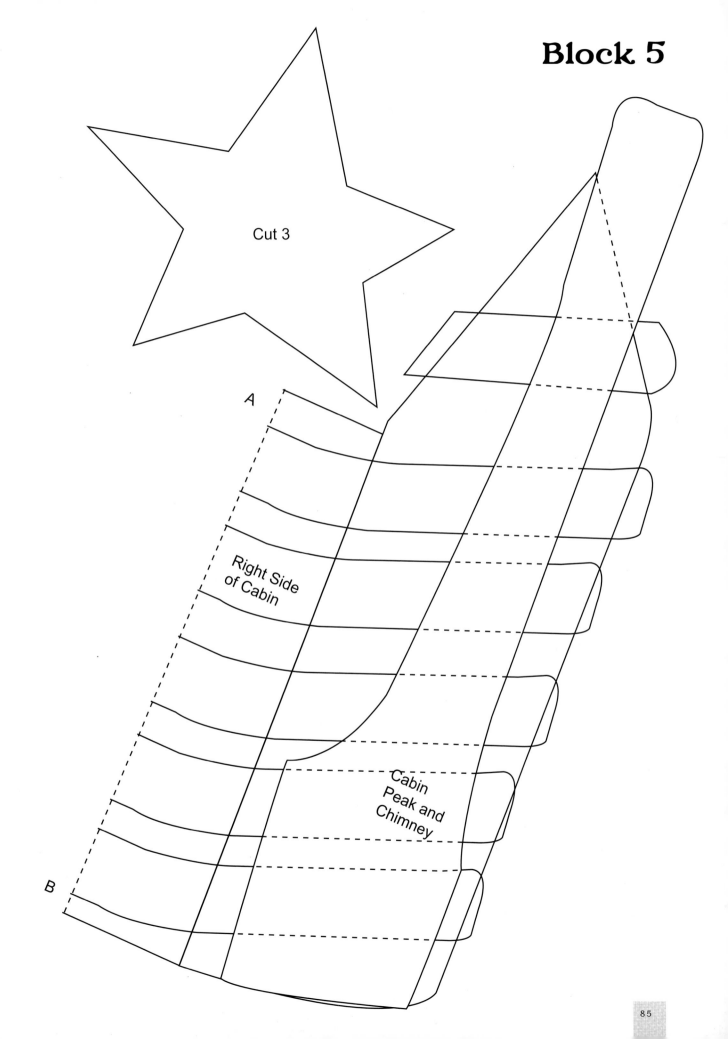

Block 5

Cut 3

A

Right Side
of Cabin

B

Cabin
Peak and
Chimney

Block 5

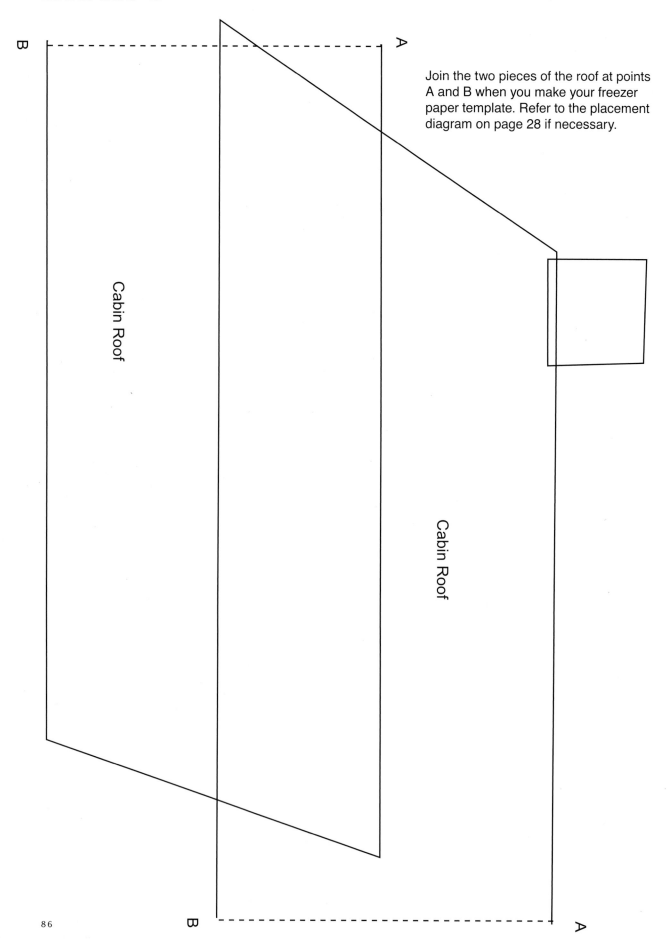

Join the two pieces of the roof at points A and B when you make your freezer paper template. Refer to the placement diagram on page 28 if necessary.

Cabin Roof

Cabin Roof

Block 5

Jan's
Leaf
Cut 15

Edie's
Leaf
Cut 13

Join the trunk at points A and B
when making your freezer paper
template. Refer to the placement
diagram on page 28 if necessary.

A B

A   B

Block 6

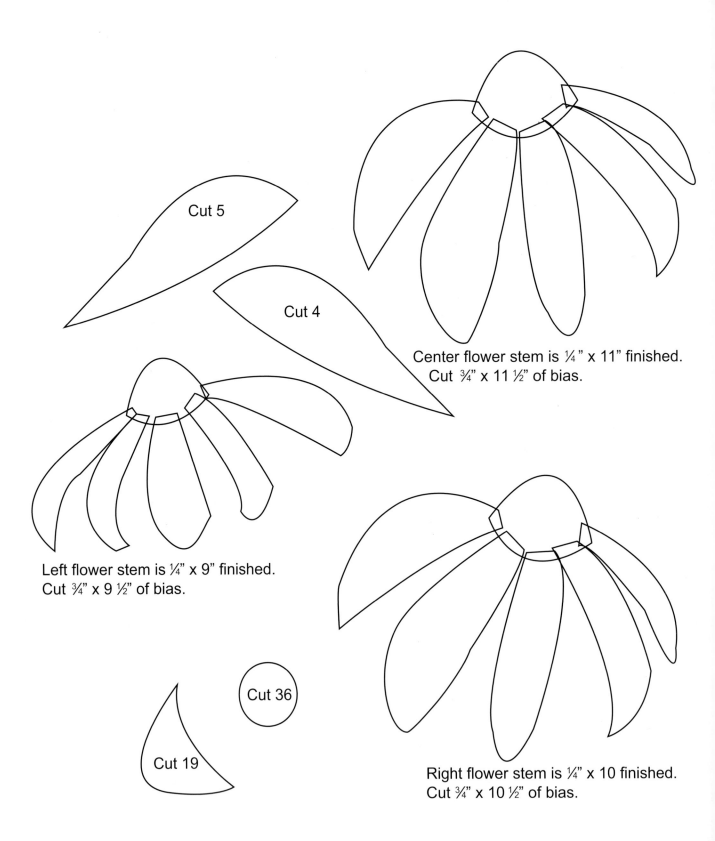

Cut 5

Cut 4

Center flower stem is ¼" x 11" finished.
Cut ¾" x 11 ½" of bias.

Left flower stem is ¼" x 9" finished.
Cut ¾" x 9 ½" of bias.

Cut 36

Cut 19

Right flower stem is ¼" x 10 finished.
Cut ¾" x 10 ½" of bias.

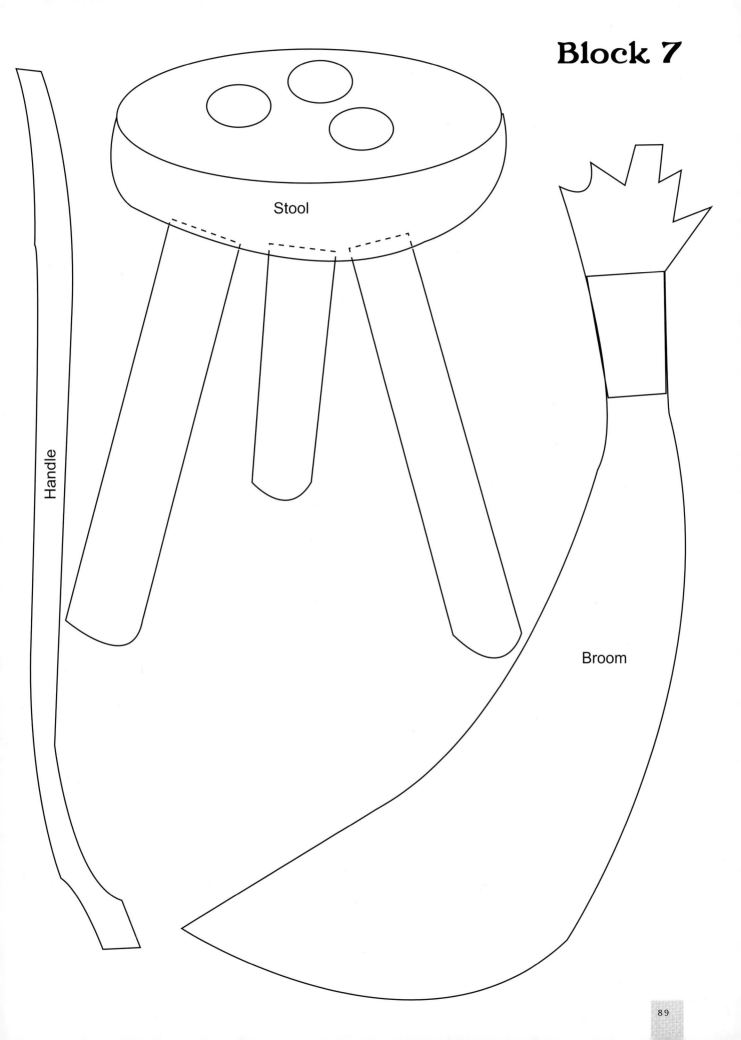

Block 7

Stool

Handle

Broom

Block 7

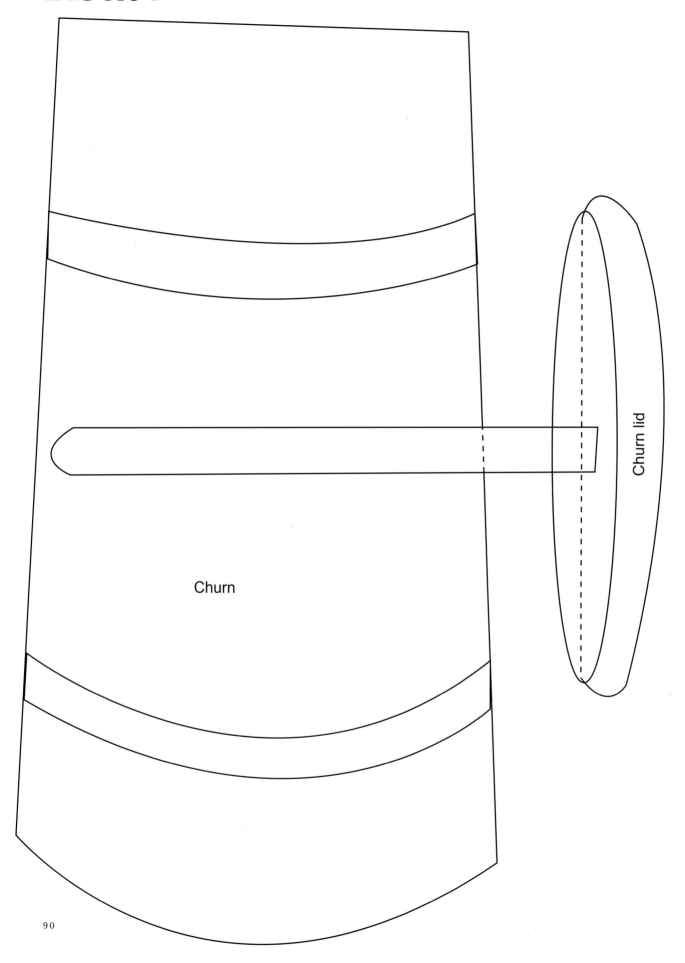

Churn

Churn lid

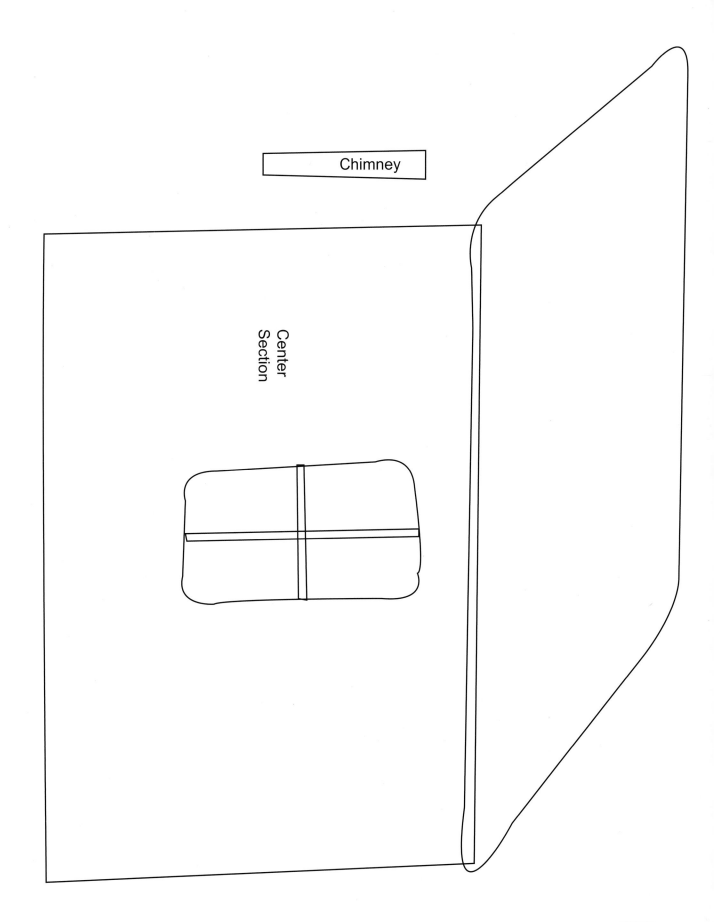

Chimney

Center
Section

Block 8

Cut 3

Right Section

Left Section

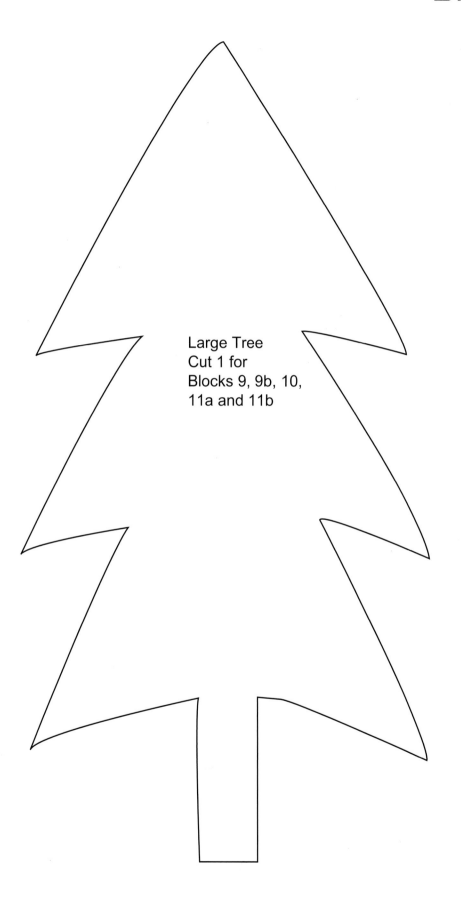

Large Tree
Cut 1 for
Blocks 9, 9b, 10,
11a and 11b

Block 9

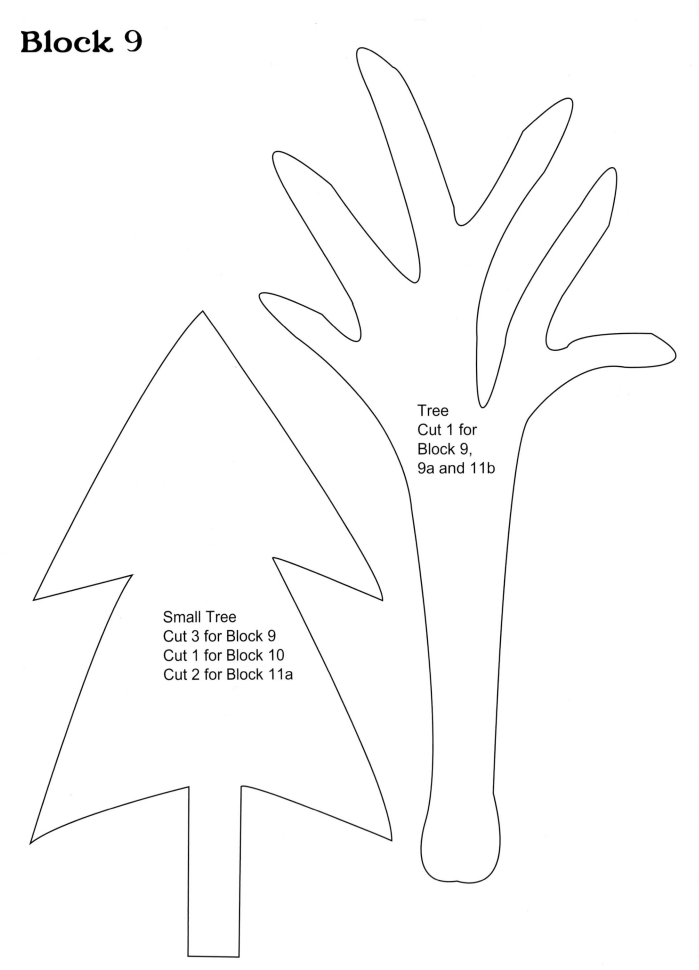

Tree
Cut 1 for
Block 9,
9a and 11b

Small Tree
Cut 3 for Block 9
Cut 1 for Block 10
Cut 2 for Block 11a

Block 10

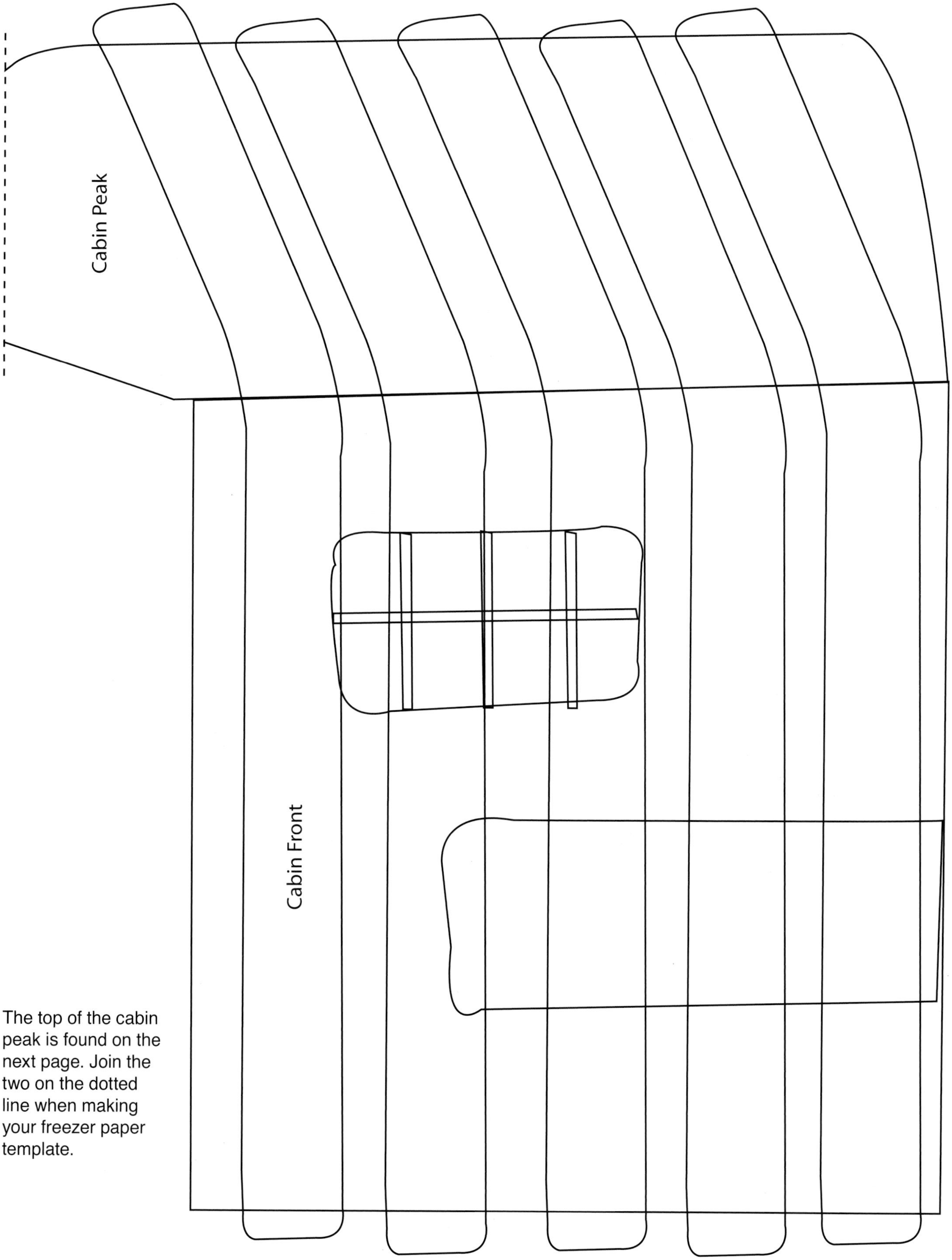

Cabin Peak

Cabin Front

The top of the cabin peak is found on the next page. Join the two on the dotted line when making your freezer paper template.

Block 10

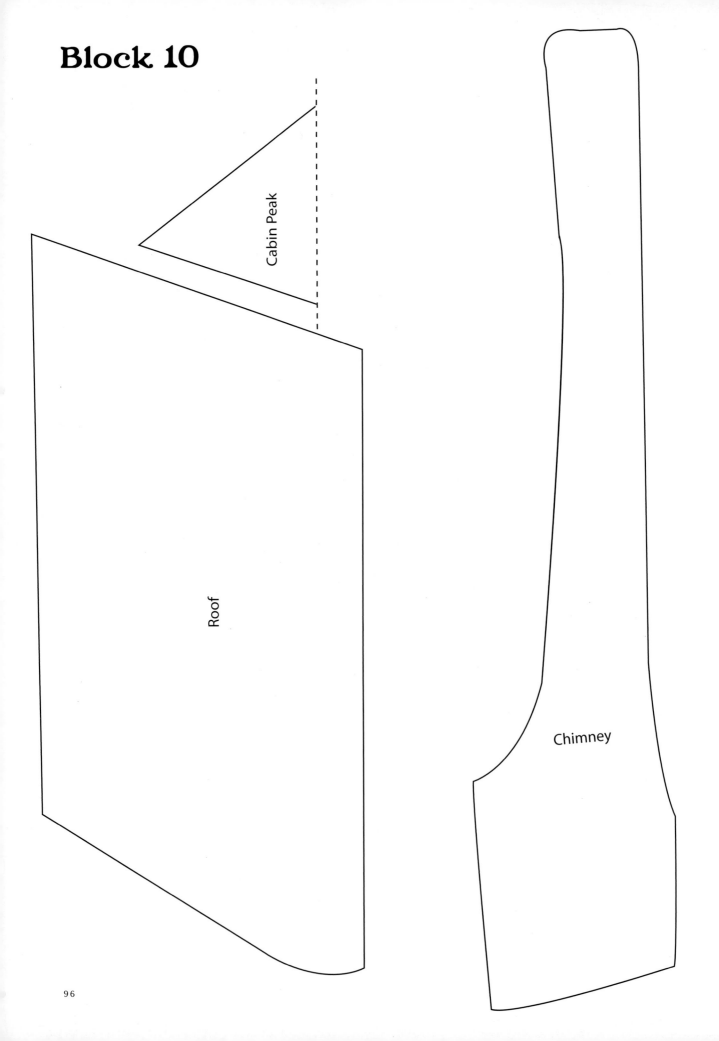

Cabin Peak

Roof

Chimney

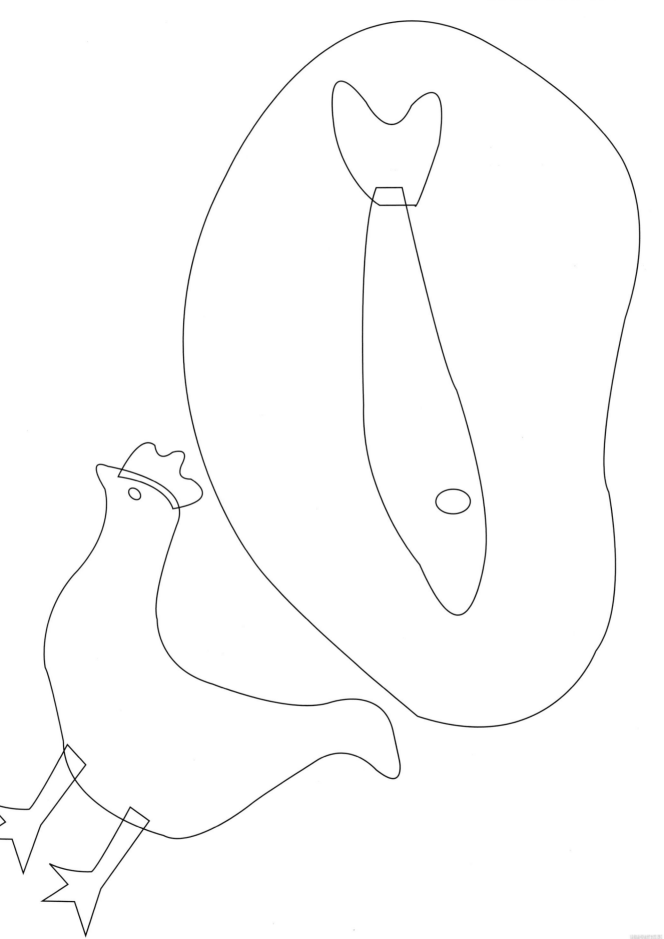

Block 11

Use these letters as a guide to draw your own initials, or go to www.pickledish.com and download a flyer with the entire alphabet.

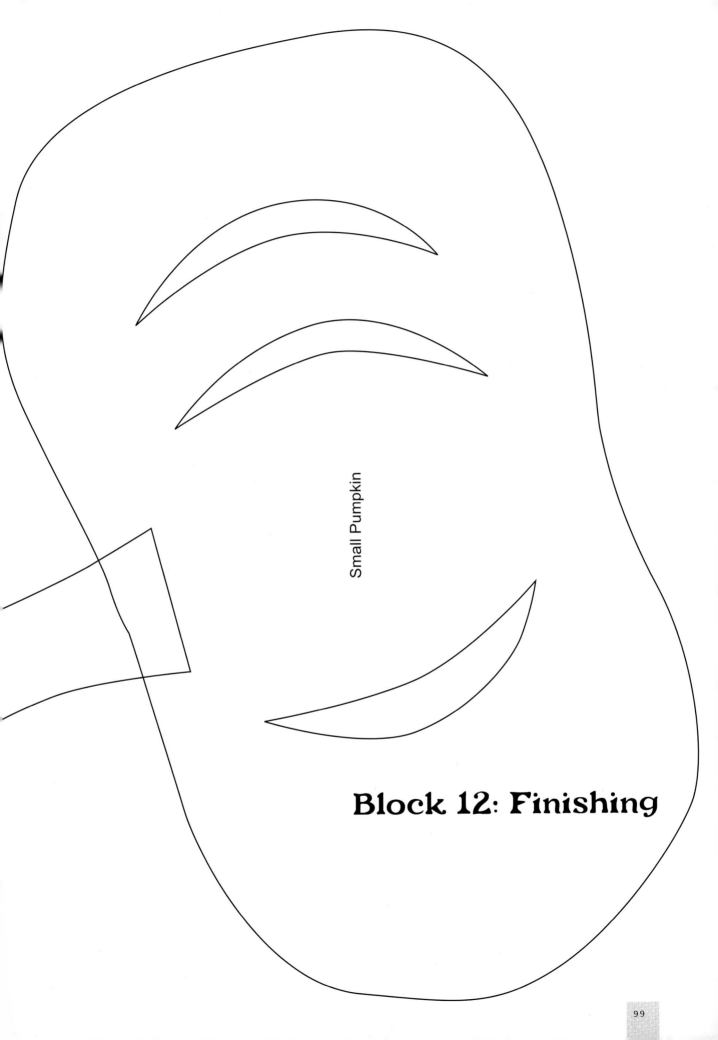

Small Pumpkin

Block 12: Finishing

Block 12: Finishing

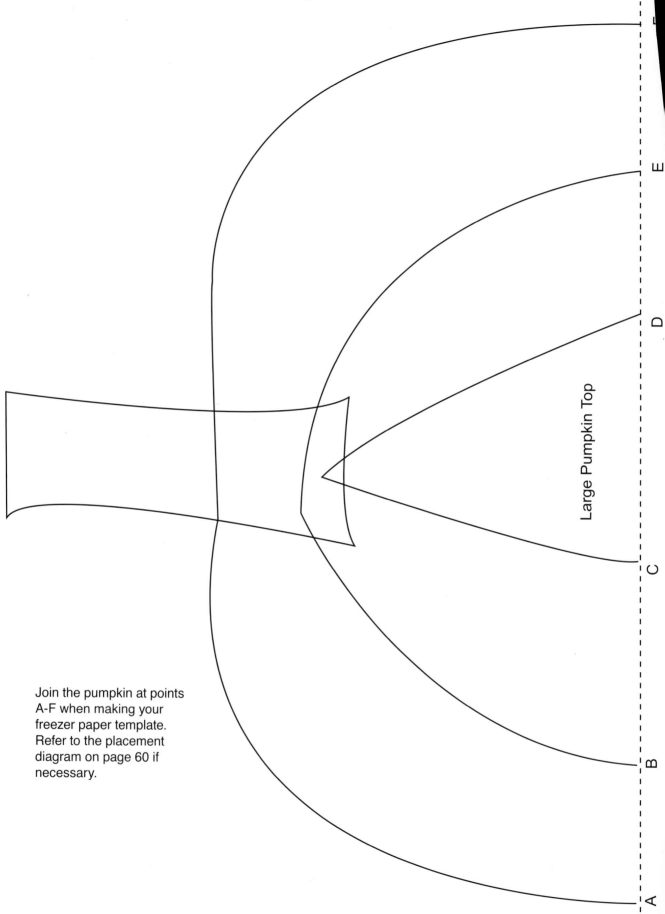

Large Pumpkin Top

Join the pumpkin at points A-F when making your freezer paper template. Refer to the placement diagram on page 60 if necessary.

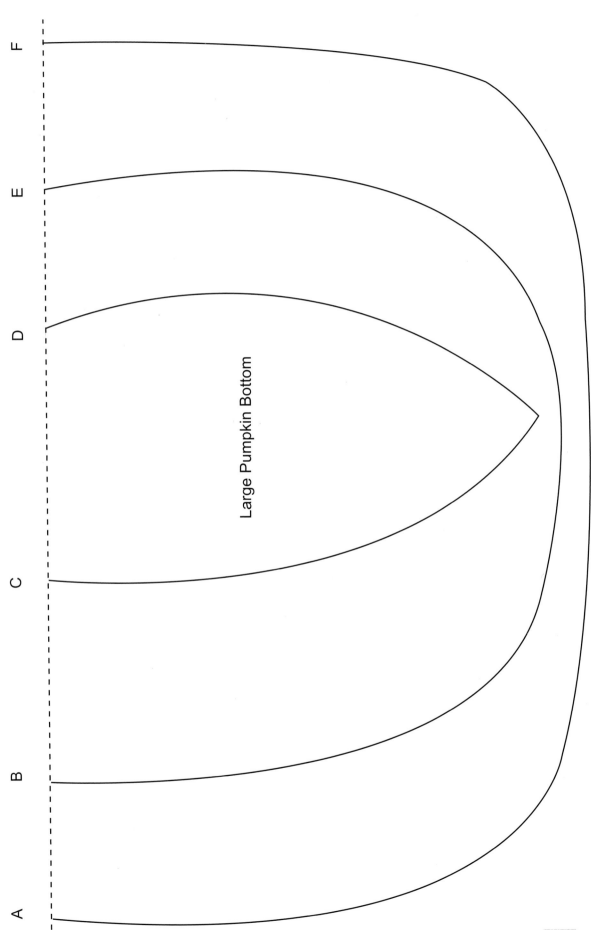

Large Pumpkin Bottom

A B C D E F

Block 12: Finishing

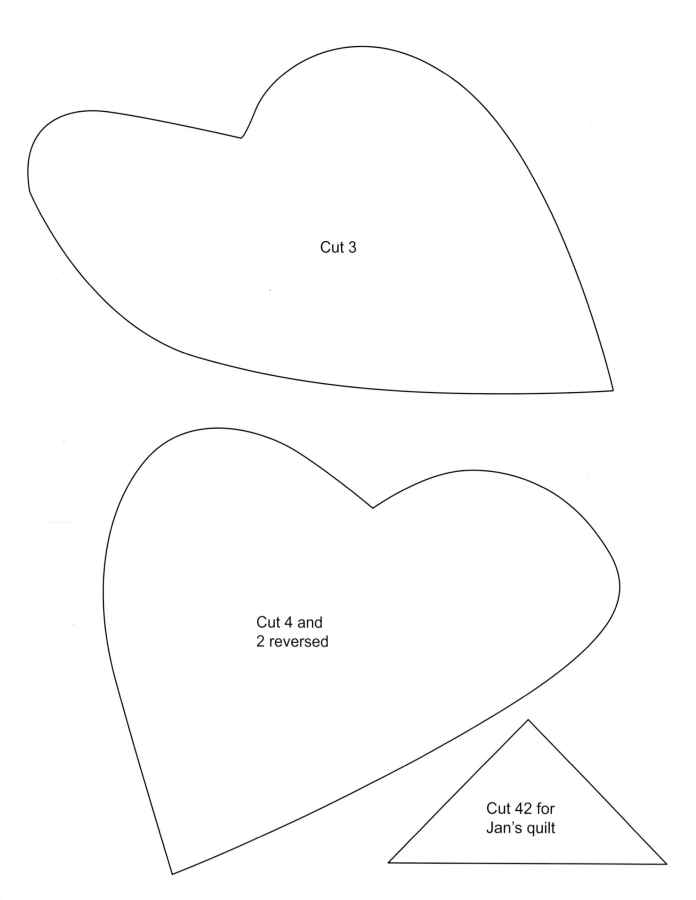

Cut 3

Cut 4 and
2 reversed

Cut 42 for
Jan's quilt

Summer Nights Templates

Cut 6

The basket base will tuck under the basket body
as indicated with the dotted line.

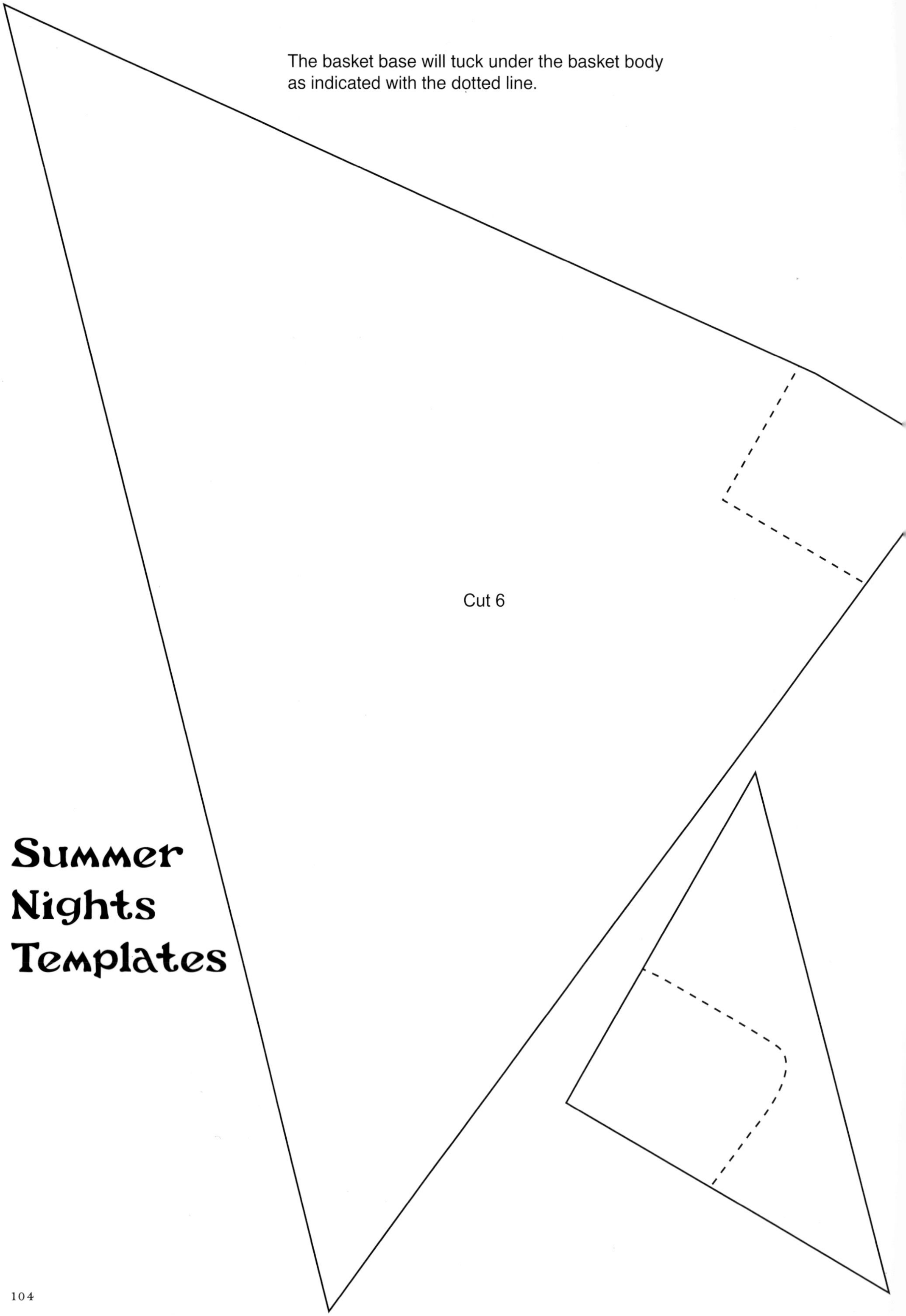

Cut 6

**Summer
Nights
Templates**

Church Bells in the Snow Templates

Join the tree t[...]
tree top on the[...]
(See page 71.[)]

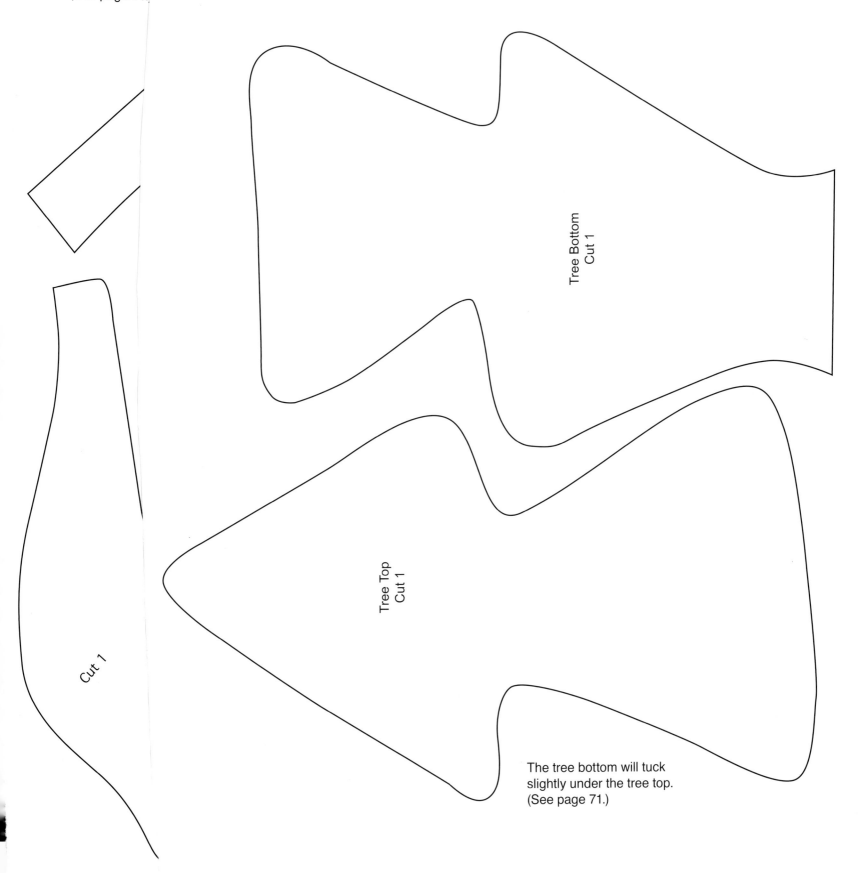

Tree Bottom
Cut 1

Tree Top
Cut 1

Cut 1

The tree bottom will tuck
slightly under the tree top.
(See page 71.)

Chu
in tl
Tem

Church Bells
in the Snow
Templates

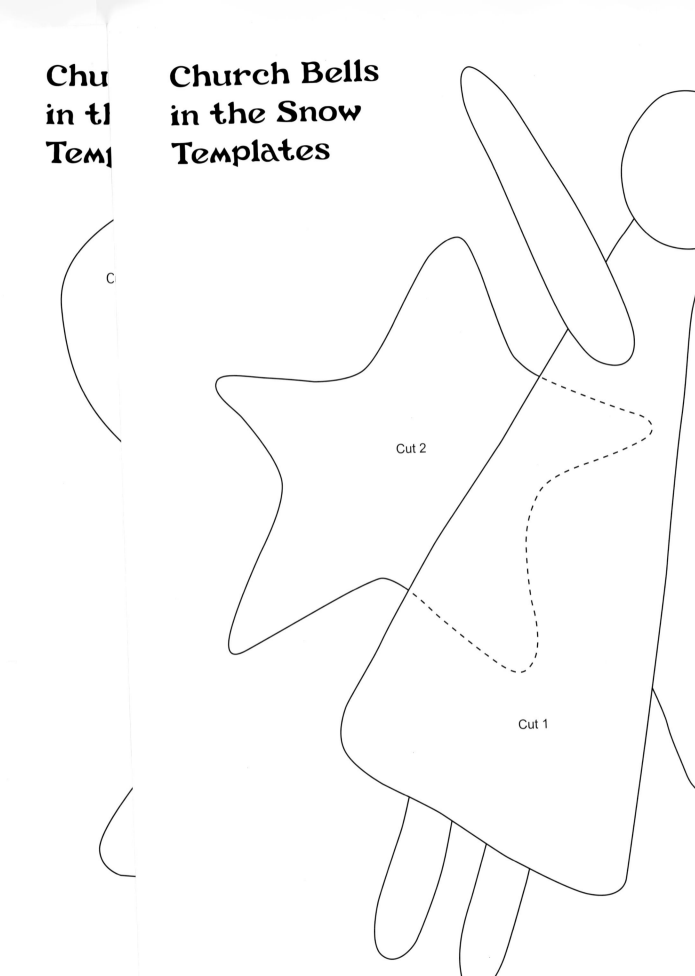

Cut 2

Cut 1

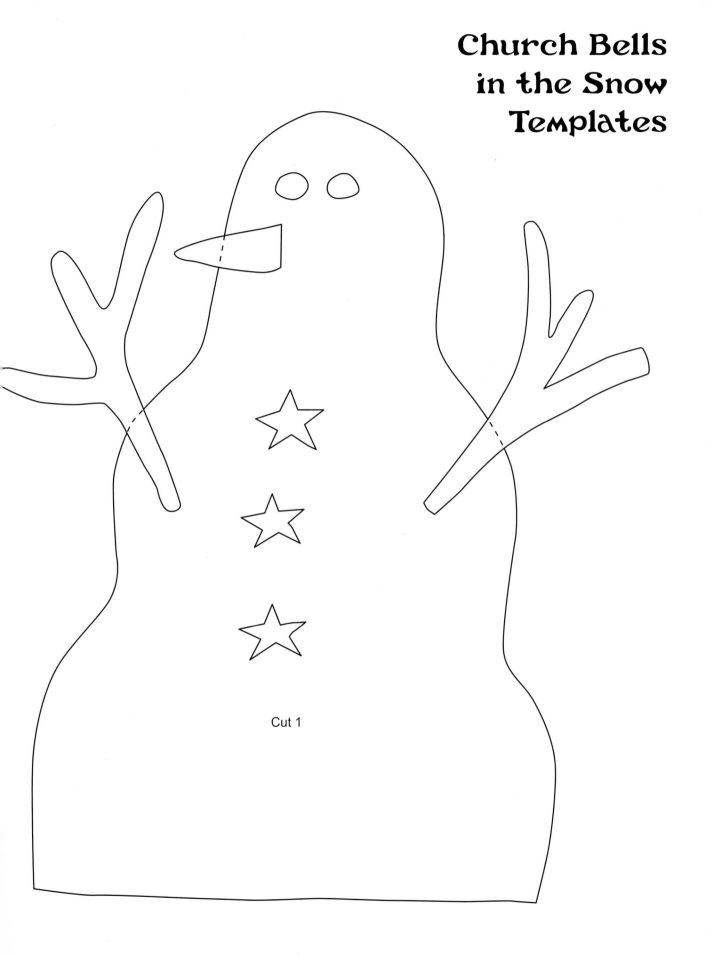

Cut 1

Church Bells in the Snow Templates

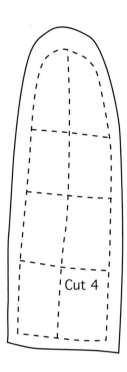

Cut 4

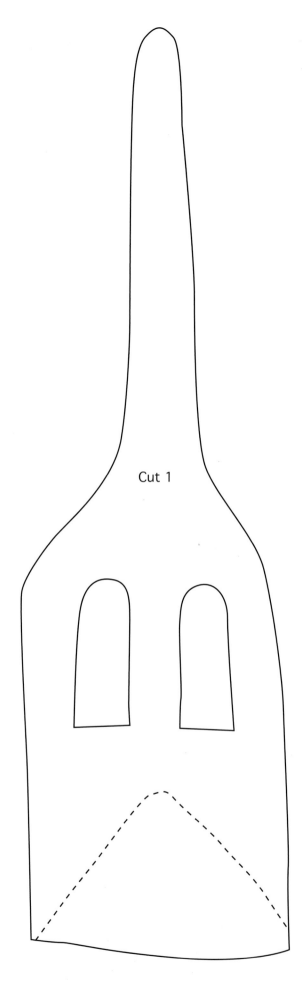

Cut 1

A template for the side of the church is not provided. Cut a rectangle 9" x 5¾" and appliqué the 4 church windows onto it before appliquéing to the background. This measurement includes seam allowance. The steeple will tuck under the peak of the Church front, found on the next page.

Church Bells in the Snow Templates

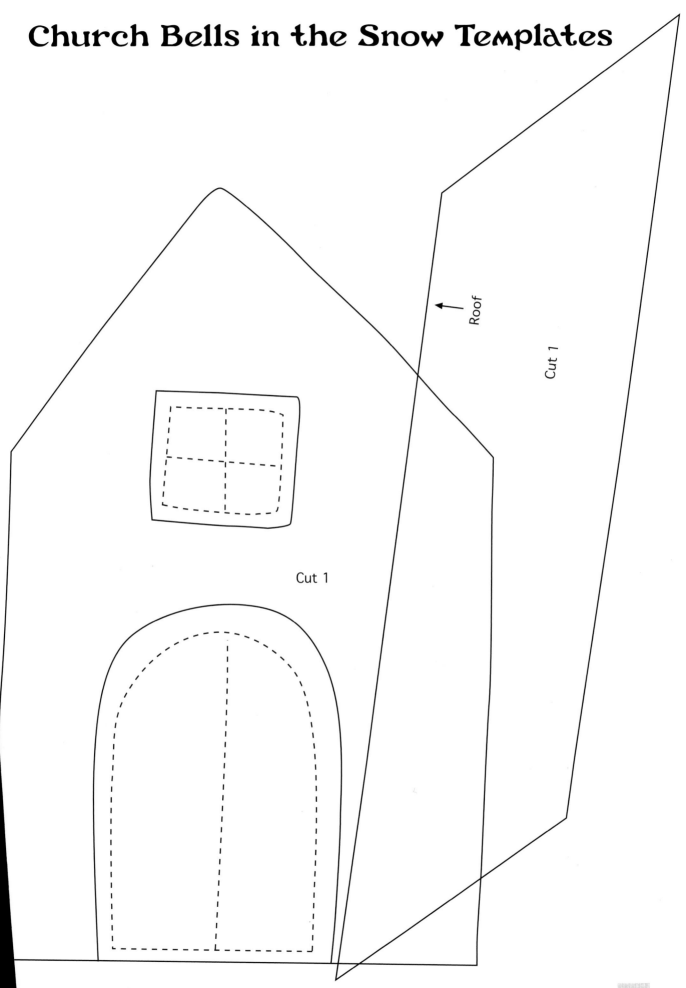

Roof

Cut 1

Cut 1

Works Cited

American Memory from the Library of Congress – Home Page. Web. 19 July 2010. <http://memory.loc.gov/>.

Armitage, Susan H., and Elizabeth Jameson. *The Women's West.* Norman: University of Oklahoma, 1987. Print.

"Bethenia Angeline Owens. Biographical Sketch." *Charles C. Chaney's Dameron-Damron Family Association Page.* Web. 19 July 2010. <http://ddfa.org/BOwensMD.htm>.

"Bethenia Owens-Adair (1840-1926)." *Oregon Encyclopedia – Oregon History and Culture.* Web. 19 July 2010. <http://www.oregonencyclopedia.org/entry/view/bethenia_owens_adair_1840_1926/>.

"Biddy Mason Biography." *Lakewood Public Library (Lakewood, Ohio).* Web. 19 July 2010. <http://www.lkwdpl.org/wihohio/maso-bid.htm>.

"Bridget "Biddy" Mason." *Women's Biographies: Distinguished Women of Past and Present.* Web. 19 July 2010. <http://www.distinguishedwomen.com/biographies/mason-b.html>.

Brown, Dee Alexander. *The Gentle Tamers: Women of the Old Wild West.* Lincoln, NE: University of Nebraska, 1981. Print.

Crutchfield, James Andrew. *The Way West: True Stories of the American Frontier.* New York: Forge, 2005. Print.

"Dame Shirley" Describes Life at a California Gold Mining Camp in the Sierra Nevada Mountains, 1851." *History Matters: The U.S. Survey Course on the Web.* Web. 19 July 2010. <http://historymatters.gmu.edu/d/6516/>.

Drewry, Jennifer M. "Stagecoach Mary Fields." *Cascade Montana Community Web Site.* Web. 19 July 2010. <http://www.cascademontana.com/mary.htm>.

Enss, Chris. *Hearts West: True Stories of Mail Order Brides on the Frontier.* Guilford, CT: TwoDot, 2005. Print.

"Frontier Women: Hardships & Triumphs." *KindredTrails.com – Genealogy – Family History – Resources.* Web. 19 July 2010. <http://www.kindredtrails.com/Frontier-Women-Page1.html>.

Goerke-Shrode, Sabine. "Solano, The Way It Was." *Historical Articles of Solano County Online Database.* Web. 19 July 2010. <http://www.solanoarticles.com/history/index.php/weblog/more/luzena_wilson_sold_land_to_buck_family/>.

Holmes, Kenneth L. *Best of Covered Wagon Women.* Norman: University of Oklahoma, 2008. Print.

Idaho State University. Web. 19 July 2010. <http://www.isu.edu/~trinmich/home.html>.

Kansas Memory. Web. 19 July 2010. <http://www.kansasmemory.org/>.

"Klondike Gold Rush National Historical Park - Index2 (U.S. National Park Service)." *U.S. National Park Service - Experience Your America.* Web. 19 July 2010. <http://www.nps.gov/klgo/>.

"Letters of Mrs. Narcissa Prentiss Whitman, 1836." *XMission Internet.* Web. 19 July 2010. <http://www.xmission.com/~drudy/mtman/html/nwhitman.html>.

Mid-1850s, The. "The Real Mountain Charley." *YELLOW TULIP PRESS.* Web. 19 July 2010. <http://www.curiouschapbooks.com/Catalog_of_Curious_Chapbooks/The_Real_Mountain_Cha body_the_real_mountain_charley.html>.

Moulton, Candy Vyvey. *The Writer's Guide to Everyday Life in the Wild W* Cincinnati, OH: Writer's Digest, 1999. Print.

Museum of the City of San Francisco. Web. 19 July 2010. <http://www.sfmuseum.org/>.

"Nicodemus National Historic Site (U.S. National Park Service *U.S. National Park Service - Experience Your America.* Web. 19 July 2010 <http://www.nps.gov/nico/>.

"Notable Biographies." *Encyclopedia of World Biography.* Web. 19 July <http://www.notablebiographies.com/news/index.html>.

"One-Eyed Charley Parkhurst's Secret." *Ohio's Yesterdays.* Web. 19 2010. <http://ohiosyesterdays.blogspot.com/2008/09/charley darkey-parkhurst-pioneer.html>.

Peavy, Linda, and Ursula Smith. *Pioneer Women The Lives of Women o Frontier.* Norman: University of Oklahoma, 1996. Print.

Russell, Sheldon. *Dreams to Dust A Tale of the Oklahoma Land Rush.* Nor University of Oklahoma, 2006. Print.

Sample, Zola Bellis. *Cherokee Strip Fever.* Perkins, OK: Evans Publication, 1984. Print.

Schlissel, Lillian. *Women's Diaries of the Westward Journey.* New York: Schocken, 1982. Print.

Siems, Shirley. "Soddy Babies." *Chase County Nebraska Genealogical & Historical Website.* Web. 19 July 2010. <http://www.chasegenne.c soddybabies.htm>.

Stratton, Joanna L. *Pioneer Women: Voices from the Kansas Frontier.* New York: Simon and Schuster, 1981. Print.

U.S. National Park Service - Experience Your America. Web. 19 July 2010. <http://www.nps.gov/>.

"THE WEST - Luzena Stanley Wilson '49er." *PBS.* Web. 19 July 2010. <http://www.pbs.org/weta/thewest/resources/archives three/luzena.htm>.

"THE WEST - Marcus and Narcissa Whitman." *PBS.* Web. 19 2010. <http://www.pbs.org/weta/thewest/people/s_z/whitma htm>.

"The Women." *Goldrush World Access.* Web. 19 July 2010. <http://v goldrush.com/~joann/women.htm>.

"Women in Alaska's History - Ethel Bush Berry." *Oracle ThinkC Library.* Web. 19 July 2010. <http://library.thinkquest.org/1 Gold_Rush/ethel.html>.

"Women in History - Stagecoach Mary Fields." *Lakewood Public (Lakewood, Ohio).* Web. 19 July 2010. <http://www.lkwdpl.or wihohio/fields.htm>.

"Women of the Gold Rush." *National Postal Museum.* Web. 19 Ju <http://www.postalmuseum.si.edu/gold/women.html>.

"Women of the West--Last Updated 07/14/01." *The Overland T Page--Last Updated 12/07/02.* Web. 19 July 2010. <http://www land.com/westpers2.html>.